COLONEL CARTER'S CHRISTMAS

THE ROMANCE OF AN OLD-FASHIONED GENTLEMAN

BY

F. HOPKINSON SMITH

ILLUSTRATED BY
F. C. YOHN and A. I. KELLER

CHARLES SCRIBNER'S SONS
NEW YORK ::::::::::::::::::::1911

COLONEL CARTER'S CHRISTMAS

Copyright, 1903, by
CHARLES SCRIBNER'S SONS

THE ROMANCE OF AN OLD-FASHIONED GENTLEMAN

Copyright, 1907, by
CHARLES SCRIBNER'S SONS

To my Readers:

It will be remembered, doubtless, that the chronicles of my very dear friend, Colonel Carter (published some years ago), make mention of but one festival of importance—a dinner given at Carter Hall, near Cartersville, Virginia; the Colonel's ancestral home. This dinner, as you already know, was to celebrate two important events—the sale to the English syndicate of the coal lands, the exclusive property of the Colonel's beloved aunt, Miss Nancy Carter; and the instantaneous transfer by that generous woman of all the purchase money to the Colonel's slender bank account: a transaction which, to quote his own words as he gallantly drank her health in acknowledgment of the gift, "enabled him to provide for one of the loveliest of her sex—she who graces our boa'd—and to enrich her declining days not only with all the comforts, but with many of the luxuries she was bawn to enjoy."

Several other festivals, however, did take place: not in the days of the dear Colonel's prosperity, nor yet at Carter Hall, but in his impecunious days in New York, while he was still living in the little house on Bedford

TO MY READERS

Place within a stone's throw of the tall clock-tower of Jefferson Market. This house, you will recall, sat back from the street behind a larger and more modern dwelling, its only outlet to the main thoroughfare being through a narrow, grewsome tunnel, lighted during the day by a half-moon sawed out in the swinging gate which marked its street entrance and illumined at night by a rusty lantern with dingy glass sides.

All reference to one of these festivals—a particular and most important festival—was omitted, much to my regret, from my published chronicles, owing to the express commands of the Colonel himself: commands issued not only out of consideration for the feelings of one of the participants—a man who had been challenged by him to mortal duel, and therefore his enemy—but because on that joyous occasion this same offender was his guest, and so protected by his hospitality.

This man was no less a person than the eminent financier, Mr. P. A. Klutchem, of Klutchem, Skinham & Co., who, you will remember, had in an open office and in the presence of many mutual friends, denounced in unmeasured terms the Cartersville & Warrentown Air Line Railroad—an enterprise to which the Virginian had lent his name and which, with the help of his friend Mr. Fitzpatrick, he was then trying to finance. Not content with thus slandering the road itself, characterizing it as "beginning nowhere and

TO MY READERS

ending nowhere," Mr. Klutchem had even gone so far as to attack the good name of its securities, known as the "Garden Spot" Bonds, and to state boldly that he would not "give a yellow dog" for "enough of 'em to paper a church." The Colonel's immediate resentment of this insult; his prompt challenge to Mr. Klutchem to meet him in mortal duel; Mr. Klutchem's refusal and the events which followed, are too well known to you to need further reference here.

The death of this Mr. Klutchem some years ago decided me again to seek the Colonel's permission to lay before my readers a succinct account, first of what led up to this most important celebration, and then some of the details of the celebration itself—one of the most delightful, if not the most delightful, of all the many delightful festivals held in the Colonel's cosy quarters on Bedford Place.

My communication drew from Colonel Carter the following characteristic letter:

CARTER HALL, CARTERSVILLE, VA.,

MY DEAR MAJOR:

I have your very kind and welcome letter, and am greatly impressed by the views you hold. I was averse at the time to any reference being made to the matter to which you so kindly refer, for the reason that some men are often more sensitive over their virtues than they are over their faults.

Mr. Klutchem's death, of course, completely alters the situation, and you can make what use you please of the incidents. In this decision I have been helped by my dear Fitz, who spent

TO MY READERS

last Sunday with us on his way South to investigate a financial matter of enormous magnitude and which only a giant intellect like his own can grasp. Fitz's only fear—I quote his exact words, my dear Major,—is that "you will let Klutchem down easy instead of roasting him alive as he deserves," but then you must not mind Fitz, for he always uses intemperate language when speaking of this gentleman.

Your room is always ready for you, and if you will run down to us now, we can smother you in roses. Chad is over his cold, but the old man seems feeble at times. Aunt Nancy is out in her coach paying some visits, and doesn't know I am writing or she would certainly send you her love.

I thanked you, did I not, for all your kindness about the double sets of harness? But I must tell you again how well the leaders look in them. The two sorrels are particularly splendid. Go into Wood's some day this week and write me what you think of a carriage he has just built for me,—a small affair in which Aunt Nancy can drive to Warrentown, or I can send to the depot for a friend.

All my heart to you, my dear Major. An open hand and a warm welcome is always yours at Carter Hall.

Your ever obedient servant and honored friend,

GEORGE FAIRFAX CARTER.

With the Colonel's permission, then, I am privileged to usher you into his cosy dining-room in Bedford Place, there to enjoy the Virginian's rare hospitality.

F. HOPKINSON SMITH.

September 30, 1903.

ILLUSTRATIONS

Katy dropped her head on his shoulder again   *Frontispiece*

                                                          FACING PAGE

"*Take them upstairs and put them on my dressin'-table*" 4

Each guest had a candle alight 84

And so the picture was begun 104

"*Promise me that you will stop the whole business*" . . 172

"*It is all her doing, Phil*" 205

COLONEL CARTER'S
CHRISTMAS

COLONEL CARTER'S CHRISTMAS

I

"What am I gwine to do wid dese yere barkers, Colonel?" asked Chad, picking up his master's case of duelling pistols from the mantel. "I ain't tetched der moufs since I iled 'em up for dat Klutchem man."

"Take them upstairs, Chad, and put them away," answered the Colonel with an indignant wave of the hand.

"No chance o' pickin' him, I s'pose? Done got away fo' sho, ain't he?"

The Colonel nodded his head and kept on looking into the fire. The subject was evidently an unpleasant one.

"Couldn't Major Yancey an' de Jedge do nuffin?" persisted the old servant, lifting one of the pistols from the case and squinting into its polished barrel.

"Eve'ything that a gentleman could do was done, Chad. You are aware of that, Major?" and he turned his head towards me—the Colonel will insist on calling me "Major." "But I am not done with him yet, Chad. The next time I meet him I shall lay my cane over his back. Take them upstairs and put them on my dressin' table. We'll keep them for some gentleman at home."

The Colonel arose from his chair, picked up the decanter, poured out a glass for me and one for himself, replenished his long clay pipe from a box of tobacco within reach of his hand and resumed his seat again. Mention of Mr. Klutchem's name produced a form of restlessness in my host which took all his self-control to overcome.

"—And, Chad," The old darky had now reached the door opening into the narrow hall, the case of pistols in his hand.

"Yes, sah."

"I think you have a right to know, Chad, why I did not meet Mr. Klutchem in the open field."

Chad bent his head in attention. This had really been the one thing of all others about which this invaluable servant had been most disturbed. Before this it had been a word, a blow, and an exchange of shots at daybreak in all the Colonel's affairs—all that Chad had attended—and yet a week or more had now elapsed since this worthy darky had moulded some extra bullets for these same dogs "wid der moufs open," and until to-night the case had never even left its place on the mantel.

"I was disposed, Chad," the Colonel continued, "to overlook Mr. Klutchem's gross insult after a talk I had with Mr. Fitzpatrick, and I went all the way to the scoundrel's house to tell him so. I found him in

"Take them upstairs and put them on my dressin' table."

his chair suffe'in' from an attack of gout. I had my caa'idge outside, and offe'ed in the most co'teous way to conduct him to it and drive him to my office, where a number of his friends and mine were assembled in order that the apology I p'posed might be as impressive as the challenge I sent. He refused, Chad, in the most insolent manner, and I left him with the remark that I should lay my cane over his shoulders whenever I met him; and I *shall*."

"Well, befo' Gawd, I knowed sumpin' had been gwine on pretty hot, for I never seed you so b'ilin' as when you come home, Colonel," replied the old servant, bowing low at the mark of his master's confidence. "I spec', though, I'd better put a couple o' corks in der moufs so we kin hab 'em ready if anythin' comes out o' dis yere caanin' business. I've seen 'em put away befo' in my time," he added in a louder voice, looking towards me as if to include me in his declaration; "but they allus hab to come for 'em agin, when dey get to caanin' one another." And he patted the box meaningly and left the room.

The Colonel again turned to me.

"I have vehy few secrets from Chad, Major, and none of this kind. By the way, I suppose that yaller dog has gotten over his gout by this time."

"Don't call him names, Colonel. He will write his own for a million if he goes on. I was in Fitz's office this morning, and I hear that Klutchem and his Boston crowd have got about every share of Consolidated Smelting issued, and the boys are climbing for it.

Fitz told me it went up fifteen points in an hour. By the by, Fitz is coming up to-night."

"I am not surprised, suh,—I am not surprised at anything these Yankees do. A man who could not appreciate a gentleman's feelin's placed as I was would never feel for a creditor, suh. He thinks of nothin' but money and what it buys him, and it buys him nothin' but vulgaarity, suh."

The Colonel was in the saddle now; I never interrupt him in one of these moods. He had risen from his chair and was standing on the mat before the fire in his favorite attitude, thumbs in his armholes, his threadbare, well-brushed coat thrown wide.

"They've about ruined our country, suh, these money-grubbers. I saw the workin' of one of their damnable schemes only a year or so ago, in my own town of Caartersville. Some Nawthern men came down there, suh, and started a Bank. Their plan was to start a haalf dozen mo' of them over the County, and so they called this one the Fust National. They never started a second, suh. Our people wouldn't permit it, and befo' I get through you'll find out why. They began by hirin' a buildin' and movin' in an iron safe about as big as a hen-coop. Then they sent out a circular addressed to our prominent citizens which was a model of style, and couched in the most co'teous terms, but which, suh, was nothin' mo' than a trap. I got one and I can speak by the book. It began by sayin' that eve'y accommodation would be granted to its customers, and ended by offerin' money at the low-

COLONEL CARTER'S CHRISTMAS

est rates of interest possible. This occurred, suh, at a time of great financial depression with us, following as it did the close of hostilities, and their offer was gladly accepted. It was the fust indication any of us had seen on the part of any Yankee to bridge over the bloody chasm, and we took them at their word. We put in what money we had, and several members of our oldest families, in order to give chaaracter to the enterprise, had their personal notes discounted and used the money they got for them for various private purposes—signin' as a gaarantee of their good faith whatever papers the bank people requi'ed of them. Now, suh, what do you think happened—not to me, for I was not in need of financial assistance at the time, Aunt Nancy havin' come into possession of some funds of her own in Baltimo',—but to one of my personal friends, Colonel Powhatan Tabb, a near neighbor of mine and a gentleman of the highest standin'? Because, suh"—here the Colonel spoke with great deliberation—"his notes had not been paid on the vehy day and hour—a thing which would have greatly inconvenienced him—Colonel Tabb found a sheriff in charge of his home one mornin' and a red flag hangin' from his po'ch. Of co'se, suh, he demanded an explanation of the outrage, and some words followed of a blasphemous nature which I shall not repeat. I shall never forget my feelin's, suh, as I stood by and witnessed that outrage. Old family plate that had been in the Tabb family for mo' than a century was knocked down to anybody who would buy; and befo' night, suh, my friend was stripped of about eve'ything he owned in the world. Nothin' escaped, suh, not even the po'traits of his ancestors!"

"What became of the bank, Colonel?" I asked in as serious a tone as I could command.

"What became of it? What *could* become of it, Major? Our people were aroused, suh, and took the law into their own hands, and the last I saw of it, suh, the hen-coop of a safe was standin' in the midst of a heap of smokin' ashes. I heard that the Bank people broke it open with a sledge-hammer when it cooled off, put the money they had stolen from our people in a black caarpet-bag, and escaped. Such pi'acies, suh, are not only cruel but vulgaar. Mr. Klutchem's robries are quite in line with these men. He takes you by the throat in another way, but he strangles you all the same."

The Colonel stroked his goatee in a meditative way, reached over my chair, picked up his half-emptied wine-glass, sipped its contents absent-mindedly and said in an apologetic tone:

"Forgive me, Major, for mentionin' Mr. Klutchem's name, I have no right to speak of him in this way behind his back. I promise you, suh, that it will not occur again."

As the Colonel ceased I caught sight of Fitz's round, good-natured face, ruddy with the cold of the snowy December night, his shoe-button eyes sparkling behind his big-bowed spectacles peering around the edge of the open door. Chad had heard his well-known

COLONEL CARTER'S CHRISTMAS

brisk tread as he mounted the steps and had let him in before he could knock.

"Who are you going to kill now?" we heard Fitz ask the old darky.

"Dey was iled up for dat Klutchem man, but he done slid, the Colonel says."

"Klutchem! Klutchem!—nothing but Klutchem. I don't seem to get rid of him down town or up," Fitz blurted out as he entered the room.

The Colonel had bounded forward at the first sound of Fitz's voice, and had him now by both hands. In another minute he had slipped off Fitz's wet overcoat and was forcing him into a chair beside my own, calling to Chad in the meanwhile to run for hot water as quick as his legs could carry him, as Mr. Fitzpatrick was frozen stiff and must have a hot toddy before he could draw another breath.

"Keep still, Fitz, don't move. I'll be back in a minute," the Colonel cried, and off he went to the sideboard for the ingredients—a decanter of whiskey, the sugar-bowl, and a nutmeg-grater, all of which he placed on the mantel over Fitz's head.

The toddy made with the help of Chad's hot water, the Colonel moved his chair so that as he talked he could get his hand on Fitz's knee and said:

"What were you doing out in the cold hall talkin' to Chad, anyhow, you dear boy, with this fire burnin' and my hands itchin' for you?"

"Dodging Chad's guns. Got that same old arsenal with him, I see," Fitz answered, edging his chair nearer the fire and stretching out his hands to the blaze. "Pity you didn't fill Klutchem full of lead when you had the chance, Colonel. It would have saved some of us a lot of trouble. He's got the Street by the neck and is shaking the life out of it."

"How was it when you left, Fitz?" I asked in an undertone.

"Looked pretty ugly. I shouldn't wonder if the stock opened at 60 in the morning."

"Have you covered your shorts yet?" I continued in a whisper.

"Not yet." Here Fitz leaned over and said to me behind his hand: "Not a word of all this now to the Colonel. Only worry him, and he can't do any good."

"By the by, Colonel"—here Fitz straightened up, and with a tone in his voice as if what he really wanted to talk about was now on the end of his tongue said: "is Aunt Nancy coming for Christmas? Chad thinks she is."

The Colonel, who had noticed the confidential aside, did not reply for a moment. Then he remarked, with a light trace of impatience in his voice:

"If you have unloaded all the caares of yo' office, Fitz, I will answer yo' question, but I cannot soil the dear lady's name by bringin' it into any conversation in which that man has a part. There are some subjects no gentleman should discuss; Mr. Klutchem's affairs is one of them. I have already expressed my opinion of him both to the Major and to Chad and I have promised them both that that scoundrel's name

COLONEL CARTER'S CHRISTMAS

shall never again pass my lips. Oblige me by never mentionin' it. Forgive me, Fitz. There's my hand. You know I love you too well for you to think that I say this in anythin' but kindness. Let me put a little mo' whiskey in that toddy, Fitz—it lacks color. So—that's better. Aunt Nancy did you ask about, my dear Fitz?—of co'se, she's comin'. And, Major,—did I tell you"—here the Colonel turned to me—"that she's going to bring a servant with her this time? The dear woman is gettin' too old to travel alone, and since Chad has been with me she has felt the need of some one to wait upon her. She has passed some weeks or mo' in Richmond, she writes, and has greatly enjoyed the change. Make no engagement for Christmas, either one of you. That loveliest of women, suh, will grace our boa'd, and it is her special wish that both of you be present."

Fitz crushed the sugar in his glass, remarked that there was not the slightest doubt of *his* being present, winked at me appreciatingly over the edge of the tumbler, rubbed his paunch slowly with one hand, and with eyes upcast took another sip of the mixture.

The Virginian to Fitz was a never-ending well of pleasure. The Colonel's generosity, his almost Quixotic sense of honor, his loyalty to his friends, his tenderness over Chad and his reverence and love for that dear Aunt—who had furnished him really with all the ready money he had spent for years, and who was at the moment caring for the old place at Cartersville while the Colonel was in New York endeavoring to float, through

COLONEL CARTER'S CHRISTMAS

Fitz, the bonds of the Cartersville & Warrentown Railroad—excited not only Fitz's admiration and love, but afforded the broker the pleasantest of contrasts to the life he led in the Street, a contrast so delightful that Fitz seldom missed at least an evening's salutation with him. That not a shovel of earth had yet been dug on the line of the Colonel's Railroad, and that the whole enterprise was one of those schemes well nigh impossible to finance, made no difference to Fitz. He never lost an opportunity to work off the securities whenever there was the slightest opening. The bonds, of course, had not been issued; they had never been printed, in fact. These details would come later,—whenever the capitalist or syndicate should begin to look into the enterprise in earnest.

Up to the moment when this whirl had caught the Street—an event which Klutchem acting for his friends had helped—Fitz had never quite given up the hope that somehow, or in some way, or by some hook or crook, some deluded capitalist, with more money than brains, would lose both by purchasing these same "Garden Spots" as the securities of the Colonel's proposed road were familiarly called in the Street. That but one single inquiry had thus far ever been made, and that no one of his or anybody else's customers had ever given them more than a hasty dismissal, had never discouraged Fitz.

As for the Colonel he was even more sanguine. The dawn of success was already breaking through the darkness and his hopes would soon be realized. Hour

COLONEL CARTER'S CHRISTMAS

after hour he would sit by his fire, building fairy castles in its cheery coals. Almost every night there was a new picture. In each the big bridge over the Tench was already built, bearing his double track road to Warrentown and the sea—he could see every span and pier of it; the town of Fairfax, named after his ancestors, was crowning the plateau; the round-house for his locomotives was almost complete, the wharves and landing docks finished. And in all of these pictures, warm and glowing, there was one which his soul coveted above all others—the return of the proud days of the old Estate: the barns and outbuildings repaired; the fences in order; Carter Hall restored to its former grandeur, and dear Aunt Nancy once more in her high spring coach, with Chad standing by to take her shawl and wraps. These things, and many others as rose colored and inspiring, the Colonel saw night after night in the glow and flash and sparkle of his wood fire.

No wonder then that Fitz kept hoping against hope; deluding him with promises and keeping up his spirits with any fairy tale his conscience would permit his telling or his ingenuity contrive.

To-night, however, Fitz's nerve seemed to have failed him. To the Colonel's direct inquiry regarding the slight nibble of an English syndicate—(that syndicate which some months later made the Colonel's fortune and with which Fitz had buoyed up his hopes) the broker had only an evasive answer. The Colonel noticed the altered tone and thought he had divined the cause.

COLONEL CARTER'S CHRISTMAS

"You are tired out, Fitz. Isn't it so? I don't wonder when I think of the vast commercial problems you are solvin' every day. Go upstairs, my dear boy, and get into my bed for the night. I won't have you go home. It's too cold for you to go out and the snow is driftin' badly. I'll take the sofa here."

"No, Colonel, I think I'll toddle along home. I am tired, I guess. I ought to be; I've had nothing but hard knocks all day."

"Then you shan't leave my house, suh; I won't permit it. Chad, go upstairs and get Mr. Fitzpatrick's chamber ready for the night, and Chad——"

Fitz laughed. "And have you sleep on that haircloth sofa, Colonel?" and he pointed to the sagging lounge.

"Why not?—I've done it befo'. Come, I insist."

Fitz was on his feet now and with Chad's assistance was struggling into his overcoat, which that attentive darky had hung over a chairback that it might dry the easier.

"I'm going home, Colonel, and to bed," Fitz said in a positive tone. "I shouldn't sleep a wink if I knew you were thrashing around on that shake-down, and you wouldn't either. Good-night"; and holding out his hand to his host, he gave me a tap on my shoulder as he passed my chair and left the room, followed by the Colonel.

It was only when the Colonel had found Fitz's rubbers himself and had turned up the collar of his coat and had made it snug around his throat to keep out

COLONEL CARTER'S CHRISTMAS

the snow, and had patted him three times on the shoulder—he only showed that sort of affection to Fitz—and had held the door open until both Fitz and Chad were lost in the gloom of the tunnel, the wind having extinguished the lantern, that the Colonel again resumed his seat by the fire.

"I must say I'm worried about Fitz, Major. He don't look right and he don't act right"—he sighed as he picked up his pipe and sank into his arm-chair until his head rested on its back. "I'm going to have him see a doctor. That's what I'm going to do, and at once. Do you know of a good doctor, Major?"

"Medicine won't help him, Colonel," I answered. I knew the dear old fellow would not sleep a wink even in his own bed if the idea got into his head that Fitz was ill.

"What will?"

"Money."

The Colonel looked at me in astonishment.

"What kind of money?"

"Any kind that's worth a hundred cents on the dollar."

"Why, what nonsense, Major, I'd take Fitz's check for a million."

"Klutchem won't."

"What's the scoundrel got to do with it?"

"Everything, unfortunately. Fitz is short of 10,000 shares of Consolidated Smelting, and Klutchem and his crowd have got about every share of it locked up in their safes. Some of Fitz's customers have gone back on him, and he's got to make the fight alone. If smelting goes up another fifteen points to-morrow Fitz goes with it. It's not a doctor he wants, it's a banker. Cash, not pills, is what will pull Fitz through."

Had a bomb been exploded on the hearth at his feet the Colonel could not have been more astonished. He sat staring into my eyes as I unfolded the story, his face changing with every disclosure; horror at the situation, anger at the man who had caused it, and finally—and this dominated all the others—profound sympathy for the friend he loved. He knew something of the tightening of the grasp of a man like Klutchem and he did not underestimate the gravity of the situation. What Consolidated Smelting represented, or what place it held in the market were unknown quantities to the Colonel. What he really saw was the red flag of the auctioneer floating over the front porch of that friend in Virginia whom the Bank had ruined, and the family silver and old portraits lying in the carts that were to take them away forever. It was part of the damnable system of Northern finance and now Fitzpatrick was to suffer a similar injustice.

"Fitz in Klutchem's power! My God, suh!" he burst out at last, "you don't tell me so! And Fitz never told me a word about it. My po' Fitz! My po' Fitz!" he added slowly with quivering lips. "Are you quite sure, Major, that the situation is as serious as you state it?"

"Quite sure. He told me so himself. He wanted

COLONEL CARTER'S CHRISTMAS

me to keep still about it, but I didn't want you to think he was ill."

"You did right, Major. I should never have forgiven you if you had robbed me of the opportunity of helpin' him. It's horrible; it's damnable. Such men as Klutchem, suh, ought to be drawn and quartered."

For an instant the Colonel leaned forward, his elbows on his knees, and looked steadily into the fire; then he said slowly with a voice full of sympathy, and in a tone as if he had at last made up his mind:

"No, I won't disturb the dear fellow to-night. He needs all the sleep he can get."

The Colonel was still in his chair gazing into the fire when I left. His pipe was out; his glass untasted; his chin buried in his collar.

"My po' Fitz!" was all he said as he lifted his hand and pressed my own. "Good-night, Major."

When I had reached the hall door he roused himself, called me back and said slowly and with the deepest emotion:

"Major, I shall help Fitz through this in the mornin' if it takes eve'y dollar I've got in the world. Stop for me as you go down town and we will call at his office together."

II

Fitz had not yet arrived when the Colonel in his eagerness stepped in front of me, and peered through the hole in the glass partition which divided Fitz's inner and outer offices.

"Come inside, Colonel, and wait—expect him after a while," was the reply from one of the clerks,—the first arrival.

But the Colonel was too restless to sit down, and too absorbed even to thank the young man for his courtesy or to accept his invitation. He continued pacing up and down the outer office, stopping now and then to note the heap of white ribbons tangled up in a wicker basket—records of the disasters and triumphs of the day before,—or to gaze silently at the large map that hung over the steam-heater, or to study in an aimless way the stock lists skewered to the wall.

He had risen earlier than usual and had dressed himself with the greatest care and with every detail perfect. His shoes with their patches, one on each toe, were polished to more than Chad's customary brilliancy; his gray hair was brushed straight back from his forehead, its ends overlapping the high collar behind; his goatee was twisted to a fish-hook point and curled outward from his shirt-front; his moustache was smooth and carefully trimmed.

COLONEL CARTER'S CHRISTMAS

The coat,—it was the same old double-breasted coat, of many repairs—was buttoned tight over his chest giving his slender figure that military air which always distinguished the Virginian when some matter of importance, some matter involving personal defence or offence, had to be settled. In one hand he carried his heavy cane with its silver top, the other held his well-brushed hat.

"What has kept Fitz?" he asked with some anxiety.

"Nothing, Colonel. Board doesn't open till ten o'clock. He'll be along presently," I answered.

Half an hour passed and still no Fitz. By this time I, too, had begun to feel nervous. This was a day of all others for a man in Fitz's position to be on hand early.

I interviewed the clerk privately.

"Stopped at the Bank," he said in an undertone. "He took some cats and dogs up with him last night and is trying to get a loan. Going to rain down here to-day, I guess, and somebody'll get wet. Curb market is steady, but you can't tell anything till the Board opens."

At ten minutes before ten by the clock on the wall Fitz burst into the office, pulled a package from inside his coat, thrust it through the hole in the glass partition, whispered something to a second clerk who had just come in, and who at Fitz's command grabbed up his hat, and with three plunges was through the doorway and racing down the street. Then Fitz turned and saw us.

COLONEL CARTER'S CHRISTMAS

"Why, you dear Colonel, where the devil did you come from?"

The Colonel did not answer. He had noticed Fitz's concentrated, business-like manner, so different from his bearing of the night before, and had caught the anxious expression on the clerk's face as he bounded past him on his way to the street. It was evident that the situation was grave and the crisis imminent. The Colonel rose from his seat and held out his hand, his manner one of the utmost solemnity.

"I have heard all about it, Fitz. I am here to stand by you. Let us go inside where we can discuss the situation quietly."

Fitz looked at the clock—it was a busy day for him—shook the Colonel's hand in an equally impressive manner, glanced inquiringly at me over his shoulder, and we all three entered the private office and shut the door: he would give us ten minutes at all events. What really perplexed Fitz at the moment was the hour of the Colonel's visit and his reference to the "stand-by." These were mysteries which the broker failed to penetrate.

The Colonel tilted his silver-topped cane against Fitz's desk, put his hat on a pile of papers, drew his chair close and laid his hand impressively on Fitz's arm. He had the air of a learned counsellor consulting with a client.

"You are too busy, Fitz, to go into the details, and my mind is too much occupied to listen to them, but

COLONEL CARTER'S CHRISTMAS

just give me an outline of the situation so that I can act with the main facts befo' me."

Fitz looked at me inquiringly; received my helpless shrug as throwing but little light on the matter, and as was his invariable custom, fell instantly into the Colonel's mood, answering him precisely as he would have done a brother broker in a similar case.

"It is what we call a 'squeeze,' Colonel. I'm through for the day, I hope, for my bank has come to my rescue. My clerk has just carried up a lot of stuff I managed to borrow. But you can't tell what to-morrow will bring. Looks to me as if everything was going to Bally-hack, and yet there are some things in the air that may change it over night."

"Am I right when I say that Mr. Klutchem is leadin' the attack? And on you?"

"That's just what he is doing—all he knows how."

"And that any relief must be with his consent?"

"Absolutely, for, strange to say, some of my defaulting customers have been operating in his office."

The Colonel mused for some time, twisting the fish-hook end of his goatee till it looked like a weapon of offence.

"Is he in town?"

"He was yesterday afternoon."

The Colonel rose from his chair with a determined air and pulled his coat sleeves over his cuffs.

"I'll call upon him at once."

Fitz's expression changed. Once start the dear Colonel on a mission of this kind and there was no telling what complications might ensue.

"He won't see you."

"I have thought of that, Fitz. I do not forget that I informed him I would lay my cane over his back the next time we met, but that mattuh can wait. This concerns the welfare of my dea'est friend and takes precedence of all personal feelin's."

"But, Colonel, he would only show you the door. He don't want *talk*. He wants something solid as a margin. I've sent it to him right along for their account, and he'll get what's coming to him to-day, but *talk* won't do any good."

"What do you mean by somethin' solid, Fitz?"

"Gilt-edged collateral,—5.20's or something as good."

"I presume any absolutely safe security would answer?"

"Yes."

"And of what amount?"

"Oh, perhaps fifty thousand,—perhaps a hundred. I'll know to-morrow."

The Colonel communed with himself for a moment, made a computation with his lips assisted by his fingers, and said with great dignity:

"You haven't had my 'Garden Spots' bonds printed yet, have you?"

"No."

"Nothin' lookin' to'ards it?"

COLONEL CARTER'S CHRISTMAS

"Yes, certainly, but nothing definite. I've got the proposition I told you about from the Engraving Company. Here it is." And Fitz pulled out a package of papers from a pigeon-hole and laid the letter before the Colonel. It was the ordinary offer agreeing to print the bonds for a specified sum, and had been one of the many harmless dodges Fitz had used to keep the Colonel's spirits up.

The Colonel studied the document carefully.

"When I accept this, of co'se, the mattuh is closed between me and the Company?"

"Certainly."

"And no other party could either print or receive the bonds except on my written order?"

"No." Fitz was groping now in the dark. Why the Colonel should have suddenly dropped Consolidated Smelting to speak of the "Garden Spots" was another mystery.

"And I have a right to transfer this order to any one I please?"

"Of course, Colonel." The mystery was now impenetrable.

"You have no objection to my takin' this letter, Fitz?"

"Not the slightest."

The Colonel walked to the window, looked out for a moment into the street, walked back to Fitz's desk, and with a tinge of resignation in his voice as if he had at last nerved himself for the worst, laid his hand on Fitz's shoulder:

COLONEL CARTER'S CHRISTMAS

"I should never have a moment's peace, Fitz, if I did not exhaust every means in my power to ward off this catastrophe from you. Kindly give me a pen."

I moved closer. Was the Colonel going to sign his check for a million, or was there some unknown friend who, at a stroke of his pen, would come to Fitz's rescue?

The Colonel smoothed out the letter containing the proposition of the Engraving Company, tried the pen on his thumbnail, dipped it carefully in the inkstand, poised it for an instant, and in a firm round hand wrote across its type-written face the words:

"Accepted.
GEORGE FAIRFAX CARTER,
of Cartersville."

Then he folded the paper carefully and slipped it into his inside pocket.

This done, he shook Fitz's hand gravely, nodded to me with the air of a man absorbed in some weighty matter, picked up his cane and hat and left the office.

"What in the name of common-sense is he going to to do with that, Fitz?" I asked.

"I give it up," said Fitz. "Ask me an easy one. Dear old soul, isn't he lovely? He's as much worried over the market as if every dollar at stake was his own. Now you've got to excuse me, Major. I've got a land-office business on hand to-day."

The Colonel's manner as he left the room had been so calm and measured, his back so straight, the swing of his cane so rhythmical, his firm military tread so full of courage and determination, that I had not followed him. When he is in these moods it is best to let him have his own way. Fitz and I had discovered this some days before, when we tried to dissuade him from planting into Klutchem's rotundity the bullets which Chad had cast with so much care.

Had I questioned him as he walked out this morning he would doubtless have said, "I do not expect you Nawthern men, with yo'r contracted ideas of what constitutes a man's personal honor, to understand the view I take of this mattuh, Major, but my blood requires it. I never forget that I am a Caarter, suh,—and you must never forget it either."

Moreover, had I gone with him the visit might have assumed an air of undue importance. There was nothing therefore for me to do but to wait. So I buried my self in an arm-chair, picked up the morning papers, and tried to possess my soul in patience until the Colonel should again make his appearance with a full report of his mission.

Twice during my long wait Fitz burst in, grabbed up some papers from his desk and bounded out again, firing some orders to his clerks as he disappeared through the door. He was too absorbed to more than nod to me, and he never once mentioned the Colonel's name.

About noon a customer in the outer office—there were half a dozen of them watching the ticker—handed an "extra" to the clerk, who brought it to me. Con-

COLONEL CARTER'S CHRISTMAS

solidated Smelting was up ten points; somebody had got out an injunction, and two small concerns in Broad Street had struck their colors and sent word to the Exchange that they could not meet their contracts.

Still no Colonel!

Had he failed to find Klutchem; had he been thrown out of the office or had he refrained from again visiting Fitz until he had accomplished something definite for his relief?

With the passing of the hours I became uneasy. The Colonel, I felt sure, especially in his present frame of mind, would not desert Fitz unless something out of the common had happened. I would go to Klutchem's office first, and not finding him there, I would keep on to Bedford Place and interview Chad.

"Been here?" growled Klutchem's clerk in answer to my question. "Well, I should think so. Tried to murder Mr. Klutchem. They're all up at the police station. Nice day for a muss like this when everything's kitin'! You don't know whether you're a-foot or a-horseback! These fire-eaters ought to be locked up!"

"Arrested!"

"Well, you'd a-thought so if you'd been here half an hour ago. He kept comin' in callin' for Mr. Klutchem, and then he sat down and said he'd wait. Looked like a nice, quiet old fellow, and nobody took any notice of him. When Mr. Klutchem came in—he'd been to the Clearing-house—they both went into his private office and shut the door. First thing we heard was some

COLONEL CARTER'S CHRISTMAS

loud talk and then the thump of a cane, and when I got inside the old fellow was beatin' Mr. Klutchem over the head with a stick thick as your wrist. We tried to put him out, or keep him quiet, but he wanted to fight the whole office. Then a cop heard the row and came in and took the bunch to the station. Do you know him?"

This last inquiry coming at the end of the explosion showed me how vivid the scene still was in the clerk's mind and how it had obliterated every other thought.

"Know him! I should think I did," I answered, my mind in a whirl. "Where have they taken him?"

"Where have they taken 'em, Billy?" asked the clerk, repeating my question to an assistant.

"Old Slip. You can't miss it. It's got a lamp over the door."

The Sergeant smiled when I stepped up to the desk and made the inquiry.

Yes; a man named Klutchem had made a charge of assault against one George Carter. Carter was then locked up in one of the cells and could not be interviewed without the consent of the Captain of the Precinct who would be back in a few minutes.

"Guess it ain't serious," the Sergeant added. "Couple of old sports got hot, that's all, and this old feller—"and he hunched his shoulder towards the cells—"pasted the other one over the nut with his toothpick. Step one side. Next!"

COLONEL CARTER'S CHRISTMAS

I sat down on a bench. The dear Colonel locked up in a cell like a common criminal. What would Chad say; what would Aunt Nancy say; what would Fitz say; what would everybody say? And then the mortification to him; the wounding of his pride; the disgrace of it all.

Men and women came and went; some with bruised heads, some with blackened eyes, one wearing a pair of handcuffs—a sneak thief, caught, with two overcoats. Was the Colonel sharing a cell with such people as these? The thought gave me a shiver.

A straightening-up of half a dozen policemen; a simultaneous touching of caps, and the Captain, a red-faced, black-moustached, blue-coated chunk of a man, held together at the waist by a leather belt and bedecked and be-striped with gilt buttons and gold braid, climbed into the pulpit of justice and faced the room.

I stepped up.

He listened to my story, nodded his head to a doorman and I followed along the iron corridor and stood in front of a row of cells. The Turnkey looked over a hoop of keys, turned one in a door, threw it wide and said, waving his finger:

"Inside!" These men use few words.

The Colonel from the gloom of the cell saw me first.

"Why, you dear Major!" he cried. "You are certainly a good Sama'itan. In prison and you visited me. I am sorry that I can't offer you a chair, suh, but you see that my quarters are limited. Fortunately so far I have been able to occupy it alone. Tell me of Fitz——"

"But Colonel!" I gasped. "I want to know how this happened? How was it possible that you——"

"My dear Major, that can wait. Tell me of *Fitz*. He has not been out of my thoughts a moment. Will he get through the day? I did eve'ything I could, suh, and exhausted eve'y means in my power."

"Fitz is all right. They've got out an injunction and the market is steadier——"

"And will he weather the gale?"

"I think so."

"Thank God for that, suh!" he answered, his lips quivering. "When you see him give him my dea'est love and tell him that I left no stone unturned."

"Why you'll see him in an hour yourself. You don't suppose we are going to let you stay here, do you?"

"I don't know, suh. I am not p'epared to say. I have violated the laws of the State, suh, and I did it purposely, and I'm willin' to abide the consequences and take my punishment. I should have struck Mr. Klutchem after what he said to me if I had been hanged for it in an hour. I may be released, suh, but it will not be with any taint on my honor. And now that my mind is at rest about Fitz, I will tell you exactly what occurred and you can judge for yo'self.

"When Mr. Klutchem at last arrived at his office—I had gone there several times—I said to him:

"'Don't start, Mr. Klutchem, I have come in the

COLONEL CARTER'S CHRISTMAS

interest of my friend, Mr. Fitzpatrick. And diff'ences between you and me can wait for a mo' convenient season.'

"'Come in,' he said, and he looked somewhat relieved, 'what do you want?' and we entered his private office and sat down. I then, in the most co'teous manner, went into the details of the transaction, and asked him in the name of decency that he would not crowd Fitz to the wall and ruin him, but that he would at least give him time to make good his obligations.

"'He can have it,' he blurted out, 'have all the time he wants—all of 'em can have it.' You know how coarse he can be, Major, and can understand how he said this. 'But'—and here Mr. Klutchem laid his finger alongside his nose—a vulgaar gesture, of co'se, but quite in keepin' with the man—'we want some collateral that are copper-fastened and gilt-edged all the way through'—I quote his exact words, Major.

"'I have expected that, suh,' I said, 'and I came p'epared,' and I unbuttoned my coat, took out the document you saw me sign in Fitz's office, and laid it befo' him.

"'What is this?' he said.

"'My entire interest in the Caartersville and Warrenton Air Line Railroad,' I answered. 'The whole issue of the Gaarden Spots, as you have no doubt heard them familiarly and very justly called, suh.'

"He looked at me and said:

"'Why these are not bonds—it is only an offer to print 'em,' he said.

COLONEL CARTER'S CHRISTMAS

"'I am aware of that,' I answered, 'but look at my signature, suh. I shall on your acceptance of my proposition, transfer the whole issue to you—then they become yo' absolute property.'

"'For what?' he interrupted.

"'As an offerin' for my friend, suh.'

"'What! As margin for Consolidated Smeltin'?'

"'True, suh. They are, of co'se, largely in excess of yo' needs, but Mr. Fitzpatrick is one of my dea'est friends. You, of co'se, realize that I am left penniless myself if my friend's final obligation to you should exceed their face value.'

"He got up, opened the door of a safe and said, 'Do you see that tin box?'

"'I do, suh.'

"'Do you know what is in it?'

"'I do not, suh.'

"'Full of stuff that will sell under the hammer above par. Tell Mr. Fitzpatrick if he and his customers have anythin' like that to bring it in—and look here'—and he pulled out a small drawer. 'See that watch?' I looked in and saw a gold watch, evidently a gentleman's, Major. 'That watch belonged to a customer who got short of our stock last week. It's wiped out now and a lot of other things he brought in. That's what we call *collateral* down here.'

"'I am not surprised, suh,' I answered. 'If men of yo' class can fo'ce themselves into our county; divest a man of his silver-plate and family po'traits, as was done to a gentleman friend of mine of the highest standin' in my own State by a Nawthern caarpet-bag Bank, I am not astonished that you avail yo'self of a customer's watch.' I said '*divest*' and '*avail*,' Major. I intended to say '*steal*' and '*rob*' but I checked myself in time.

"'Do you think that's any worse than yo' comin' down here and tryin' to bunco me with a swindle like that'—and he picked up the document and tossed it on the flo'.

"You know me well enough, Major, to know what followed. Befo' the words were out of his mouth he was flat on his back and I standin' over him with my cane. Then his clerks rushed in and separated us. My present situation is the result."

The Colonel stopped and looked about the prison corridor. "Strange and interestin' place, isn't it, Major? I shall be reasonably comfo'table here, I s'pose"—and he raised his eyes towards the white-washed ceiling. "There is not quite so much room as I had at City Point when I was a prisoner of war, but I shall get along, no doubt. I have not inqui'ed yet whether they will allow me a servant, but if they do I shall have Chad bring me down some comfo'ts in the mornin'. I think I should like a blanket and pillow and perhaps an easy-chair. I can tell better after passin' the night here. By the way, Major, on yo' way home you might stop and see Chad. Tell him the facts exactly as I have stated them to you. He will understand; he was with me, you remember, when I was overpow'ed and captured the last year of the War."

COLONEL CARTER'S CHRISTMAS

The Turnkey, who had been pacing up and down the corridor, stopped in front of the gate. The Colonel read the expression on his face, and shaking my hand warmly, said with the same air that a captured general might have had in taking leave of a member of his staff:

"The officer seems impatient, Major, and I must, therefo', ask you to excuse me. My dear love to Fitz, and tell him not to give my imprisonment a thought. Good-by," and he waved his hand majestically and stepped back into the cell.

III

The arrival of Fitz in a cab at the police-station half an hour later—just time enough for me to run all the way to his office—the bailing out of the Colonel much against his protest, his consent being gained only when Fitz and I assured him that such things were quite within the limit of our judicial code, and that no stain on his honor would or could ensue from any such relief; the Colonel's formal leave-taking of the Captain, the Sergeant and the Turnkey, each of whom he thanked impressively for the courtesies they had shown him; our driving—the Colonel and I—post-haste to Bedford Place, lest by any means Chad might have heard of the affair and so be frightened half out of his wits; the calm indifference of that loyal darky when he ushered us into the hall and heard the Colonel's statement, and Chad's sententious comment: "In de Calaboose, Colonel! Well, fo' Gawd! what I tell ye 'bout dis caanin' bis'ness. Got to git dem barkers ready jes' I tol' ye; dat's de only thing dat'll settle dis muss,"—these and other incidents of the day equally interesting form connecting links in a story which has not only become part of the history of the Carter family but which still serve as delightful topics whenever the Colonel's name is mentioned by his many friends in the Street.

COLONEL CARTER'S CHRISTMAS

More important things, however, than the arrest and bailing out of the Colonel were taking place in the Street. One of those financial bombs which are always lying around loose—a Pacific Mail, or Erie, or N. P.—awaiting some fool-match to start it, sailed out from its hiding-place a few minutes before the Exchange closed—while Fitz was bailing out the Colonel, in fact—hung for an instant trembling in mid-air, and burst into prominence with a sound that shook the Street to its foundations. In five minutes the floor of the Exchange was a howling mob, the brokers fighting, tearing, yelling themselves hoarse. Money went up to one per cent and legal interest over night, and stocks that had withstood every financial assault for years tottered, swayed and plunged headlong. Into the abyss fell Consolidated Smelting. Not only were the ten points of the day's rise wiped out, but thirty points besides. Shares that at the opening sold readily at 55 went begging at 30. Klutchem and his backers were clinging to the edges of the pit with ruin staring them in the face, and Fitz was sailing over the crater thousands of dollars ahead of his obligations.

The following morning another visitor—a well-dressed man with a diamond pin in his scarf—walked up and down Fitz's office awaiting his arrival—a short, thick-set, large-paunched man with a heavy jaw, a straight line of a mouth, two little restless eyes wobbling about in a pulp of wrinkles, flabby cheeks, a nose that was too small for the area it failed to ornament, and a gray stubbly beard shaven so closely at its edges that it looked as if its owner might either wear it on his chin or put it in his pocket at his pleasure.

"Down yet?" asked the visitor in a quick, impatient voice.

"Not yet, Mr. Klutchem. Take a seat." Then the clerk passed his hand over his face to straighten out a rebellious smile and hid his head in the ledger.

"I'll wait," retorted the banker, and stepping inside Fitz's private office he settled himself in a chair, legs apart, hands clasped across his girth.

Fitz entered with an air that would have carried comfort to the Colonel's soul—with a spring, a breeze, a lightness; a being at peace with all the world; and best of all with a self-satisfied repose that was in absolute contrast to the nervousness of the day before.

"Who?" he asked of his clerk.

"Klutchem."

"Where?"

The clerk pointed to the office door.

Fitz's face straightened out and grew suddenly grave, but he stepped briskly into his sanctum and faced his enemy.

"Well, what is it, Mr. Klutchem?"

Before his visitor opened his mouth, Fitz saw that the fight was all out of the Head Centre of Consolidated Smelting. A nervous, conciliatory smile started from the line of Klutchem's mouth, wrinkled the flesh of his face as far as his cheeks, and died out again.

"We got hit pretty bad yesterday, Fitzpatrick, and

COLONEL CARTER'S CHRISTMAS

I thought we might as well talk it over and see if we couldn't straighten out the market."

"Then it isn't about Colonel Carter?" said Fitz coldly.

He had all the Consolidated he wanted and didn't see where Klutchem could be of the slightest use in straightening out anything.

"I'll attend to him later," replied Klutchem, and a curious expression overspread his face. "You heard about it, then?"

"Heard about it! I bailed him out. If you wanted to lock anybody up why didn't you get after some one who knew the ropes, not a man like the Colonel who never had a dishonest thought in his head and who is as tender-hearted as a child."

"You don't know what you're talking about," flared Klutchem. "He came down with a cock-and-bull story and wanted me to take——"

"I know the whole story, every word of it. He came down to offer you every dollar of his interest in a scheme that is as real to him as if the bonds were selling on the Exchange at par. They are all he has in the world, and if some miracle should occur and they should be worth their face value he would never touch a penny of the proceeds if he was starving to death, because of the promise he made you. And in my interest, too, not his own, and all for love of me, his friend."

"But it was only a letter from a concern offering to print——"

"Certainly. And across it he had written his name —both, I grant you, not worth the paper they were written on. But why didn't you have the decency to humor the dear old fellow as we all do, and treat him with the same courtesy with which he treated you, instead of insulting him by throwing the letter in his face. You'll excuse me, Mr. Klutchem, when I say it gets me pretty hot when I think of it. I don't blame him for cracking you over the head, and neither would you, if you understood him as I do."

Klutchem looked out of the window and twisted his thumbs for an instant as if in deep thought. The outcome of the interview was of the utmost importance to him, and he did not want anything to occur which would prejudice his case with the broker. Fitz sat in front of him, bent forward, his hands on his knees, his eyes boring into Klutchem's.

Then a puzzled, and strange to say what appeared to be a more kindly expression broke over Klutchem's face.

"I guess I was rough, but I didn't mean it, really. You know how it was yesterday—regular circus all day. I wouldn't have made the charge at the police-station—for he didn't hurt me much—if the policeman hadn't compelled me. And then don't forget, this isn't the first time I've come across him. He came to my house once when I was laid up with the gout, and——"

"Yes," interrupted Fitz, "I haven't forgotten it, and what did he come for? To apologize, didn't he? I

COLONEL CARTER'S CHRISTMAS

should have thought you'd have seen enough of him at that time to know what kind of a man he was. Down here in the Street we've got to put things down on paper and we don't trust anybody. We don't understand the kind of a man whose word is literally as good as his bond, and who, to help any man he calls his friend, would spend his last cent and go hungry the balance of his life. I've lived round here a good deal in my time and I've seen all kinds of men, but the greatest compliment I ever had paid me in my life was when the Colonel offered you yesterday the scrap of paper that you threw back in his face."

As Fitz talked on Klutchem's tightly knit brows began to loosen. He hadn't heard such things for a good many years. Life was a scramble and devil take the hindermost with him. If anybody but Fitz—one of the level-headed men in the Street—had talked to him thus, he might not have paid attention, but he knew Fitz was sincere and that he spoke from his heart. The still water at the bottom of the banker's well—the water that was frozen over or sealed up, or so deep that few buckets ever reached it—began to be stirred. His anxiety over Consolidated only added another length to the bucket's chain.

"Fitzpatrick, I guess you're right. What ought I to do?"

"You ought to go up to his house this very day and beg his pardon, and then wipe out that idiotic charge you made at the police-station."

"I will, Fitzpatrick."

"You will?"

"Yes."

"There's my hand, Now bring out your Consolidated Smelting, and I'll do what's decent."

At four o'clock that same day Fitz, with Mr. Klutchem beside him, swung back the wicket-gate of the tunnel, traversed its gloom, crossed the shabby yard piled high with snow heaped up by Chad's active shovel, and rapped at the front door of the little house.

The Colonel was in his chair by the fire. I had just told him the good news, and he and I were sampling a fresh bottle of the groceryman's Madeira in celebration of the joyous turn in Fitz's affairs, when Chad with eyes staring from his head announced:

"Misser Klutchem and Misser Fitzpatrick."

What the old darky thought was coming I do not know, but I learned afterwards, that as soon as he had closed the door behind the visitors, he mounted the stairs three steps at a time, grabbed up the case of pistols from his master's dressing-table, pulled the corks from their mouths, and hurrying down laid the case and its contents on the hall table to be ready for instant use.

The announcement of Klutchem's name brought the Colonel to his feet as straight as a ramrod.

"It's all right, Colonel," said Fitz, noting the color rise in his friend's face. "Mr. Klutchem and I have settled all our differences. He has just offered me a barrel of Consolidated, and at my own price. That fight's all over, and I bear him no grudge. As to your-

COLONEL CARTER'S CHRISTMAS

self, he has come up to tell you how sorry he is for what occurred yesterday, and to make any reparation to you in his power."

Klutchem had not intended to go so far as that, and he winced a little under Fitz's allusion to the "barrel," but he was in for it now, and would follow Fitz's lead to the end. Then again, the papers in the Consolidated matter would not be signed until the morning.

"Yes, Carter, I'm sorry. Fact is, I misunderstood you. I was very busy, you remember, and I'm sorry, too, for what occurred at the police-station; that, however, you know I couldn't help."

The omission of the Virginian's title scraped the skin from the Colonel's *amour propre*, but the words "I'm sorry" coming immediately thereafter healed the wound.

The military bearing of our host began to relax.

"And you have come here with my friend Mr. Fitzpatrick to tell me this?"

"I have."

"And you intended no reflection on my honor when you—when you—handed me back my secu'ities?"

"No, I didn't. The stuff wasn't our kind, you know. If I had stopped to hear what you had to say I'd——"

"Let it all pass, suh. I accept yo' apology in the spirit in which it was given, suh. As to my imprisonment, that is a matter which is not of the slightest consequence. We soldiers are accustomed to these inconveniences, suh. It is part of the fortunes of war.

Take that chair, Mr. Klutchem, and let my servant relieve you of yo' coat and hat."

The promptness with which that individual answered to his name left no doubt in my mind that that worthy defender of the Colonel's honor had been standing ready outside the door, which had been left partly open for the purpose, his hand on the knob.

"Yes, sah. I heard ye, Colonel."

"And, Chad, bring some glasses for the gentlemen."

Klutchem settled his large frame in the chair that had been vacated by the Colonel, and watched the glass being slowly filled from a decanter held in his host's own hands. Fitz and I retired to the vicinity of the sideboard, where he gave me in an undertone an account of the events of the morning.

"Got a nice box of a place here, Colonel," remarked Mr. Klutchem. He remembered the title this time—the surroundings had begun to tell upon him. "Cost you much?" and the broker's eyes roamed about the room, taking in the big mantel, the brass andirons, India blue china and silver candlesticks.

"A mere trifle, suh," said the Colonel, stiffening. The cost of things were never mentioned in this atmosphere. "To associate bargain and sale with the appointments of yo' household is like puttin' yo' hospitality up at auction," he would frequently say.

"A mere trifle, suh," he repeated. "My estates, as you probably know, are in Virginia, near my ancestral town of Caartersville. Are you familiar with that part of the country, suh?"

COLONEL CARTER'S CHRISTMAS

And thereupon, on the banker's expressing his entire ignorance of Fairfax County and its contiguous surroundings, the Colonel, now that his honor as a duellist had been satisfied by Klutchem's apologies; his friend's ruin averted by the banker's generosity, as was attested by his offering Fitz a barrel full of securities which the day previous were worth their weight in gold; and especially because this same philanthropist was his guest, at once launched forth on the beauty of his section of the State. In glowing terms he described the charms of the river Tench; the meadows knee-deep in clover; the mountains filled with the riches of the Orient looming up into the blue; the forests of hardwood, etc., etc., and all in so persuasive and captivating a way that the practical banker, always on the lookout for competent assistants, made a mental memorandum to consult Fitz in the morning on the possibility of hiring the Colonel to work off an issue of State bonds which at the moment were dead stock on his hands.

By this time Klutchem, warmed by his host's Madeira and cheery fire, had not only become really interested in the man beside him, but had lost to a certain extent something of his blunt Wall Street manner and hard commercial way of looking at things. It was, therefore, not surprising to either Fitz or myself, who had watched the gradual adjustment of the two men, to hear the Colonel, who had now entirely forgotten all animosity towards his enemy say to Klutchem with great warmth of manner, and with the evident intention of not being outdone in generosity at such a time:

"I would like to show you that gaarden, suh. Perhaps some time I may have the pleasure of entertainin' you in my own home at Caartersville."

Mr. Klutchem caught his breath. He saw the Colonel was perfectly sincere, and yet he could not but admit the absurdity of the situation. Invited to visit the private estate of a man who had caned him the day before, and against whom he was expected in the morning to make a complaint of assault and battery!

"Oh, that's mighty kind, Colonel, but I guess you'll have to excuse me."

The banker, as he spoke, glanced at Fitz. He didn't want to do anything to offend Fitz—certainly not until the papers in the Consolidated Smelting settlement were complete and the documents signed—and yet he didn't see how he could accept.

"But I won't take no for an answer, suh. Miss Caarter will be here in a day or two, and I will only be too happy to discuss with her the date of yo' visit."

Before Klutchem could refuse again Fitz stepped forward, and, standing over Mr. Klutchem's chair, dug his knuckles into the broker's back. The signal was unmistakable.

"Well, thank you, Colonel. I'll speak to my daughter about it, and if——"

"Yo' daughter, suh? Then I am sure the last obstacle is removed. Miss Caarter will be mo' than delighted, suh, to entertain her, too. I will ascertain

COLONEL CARTER'S CHRISTMAS

my aunt's plans as soon as she arrives, and will let you know definitely when she will be best p'epared for yo' entertainment."

When the party broke up, and Fitz and Mr. Klutchem had been helped on with their coats by Chad, Klutchem remarked to Fitz as we all walked through the tunnel:

"Queer old party, Fitzpatrick; queerest I ever saw. You were right—not a crooked hair in his head. Glad I came. Of course I can't go down to his place—haven't got the time—but I bet you he'd be glad to see me if I did. Funny, too—poor as a rat and busted, and yet he never said 'Garden Spots,' once."

On my re-entering the house,—Fitz had gone on with Klutchem—Chad, who was waiting for me, took me into a corner of the hall and said in a voice filled with disappointment:

"What I tell ye, Major? Ain't dat too bad? I ain't never gwine ter forgib de Colonel for lettin' him git away. Gor-A-Mighty! Did ye see de size of him —hardly git frough de gate! Why, der warn't no chance o' missin' him. Colonel could a-filled him ful o' holes as a sieve."

IV

The Colonel's positive injunction that each one of his friends should call on every one of his guests within forty-eight hours of their arrival was never necessary in the case of Miss Ann Carter. One day was enough for me—one hour would have been more to my liking. Only consideration for her comfort, and the knowledge that she would be somewhat fatigued by her journey from Carter Hall northward, ever kept me away from her that long. Then, again, I knew that she wanted at least one entire day in which to straighten out the various domestic accounts of the little house in Bedford Place, including that complicated and highly-prized pass-book of the "Grocer-man."

And then Chad's delight when he opened the door with a sweep, his face a sunburst of smiles and announced Miss Carter's presence in the house! And the new note in the Colonel's voice—a note of triumph and love and pride! And the touches here and there inside the cosy rooms; touches that only a woman can give—a new curtain here, a pot of flowers there: all joyous happenings that made a visit to Aunt Nancy, as we loved to call her, one of the events to be looked forward to.

COLONEL CARTER'S CHRISTMAS

But it was not Chad who opened the door on this particular morning. That worthy darky was otherwise occupied; in the kitchen, really, plucking the feathers from the canvas-back ducks. They had been part of the dear lady's impedimenta, not to mention a huge turkey, a box of terrapin, and a barrel of Pongateague oysters, besides unlimited celery, Tolman sweet potatoes, and a particular brand of hominy, for which Fairfax County was famous.

I say it was not Chad at all who opened the door and took my card, but a scrap of a pickaninny about three feet high, with closely-cropped wool, two strings of glistening white teeth—*two*, for his mouth was always open; a pair of flaring ears like those of a mouse, and two little restless, wicked eyes that shone like black diamonds: the whole of him, with the exception of his cocoanut of a head, squeezed into a gray cloth suit bristling with brass buttons and worsted braid, a double row over his chest, and a stripe down each seam of his trousers.

Aunt Nancy's new servant!

The scrap held out a silver tray; received my card with a dip of his head, threw back the door of the dining-room, scraped his foot with the flourish of a clog dancer, and disappeared in search of his mistress.

Chad stepped from behind the door, his face in a broad grin. He had crept up the kitchen stairs, and had been watching the boy's performance from the rear room. His sleeves were rolled up and some of the breast feathers of the duck still stuck to his fingers.

"Don't dat beat de lan'! Major," he said to me. "Did ye see dem buttons on him? Ain't he a wonder? Clar to goodness looks like he's busted out wid brass measles. And he a-waitin' on de Mist'iss! I ain't done nothin' but split myself a-laughin' ever since he come. MY ! ! !" and Chad bent himself double, the tears starting to his eyes.

"What's his name, Chad?"

"Says his name's Jeems. *Jeems,* mind ye!" Here Chad went into another convulsion. "Jim's his real name, jes' Jim. He's one o' dem Barbour niggers. Raised down t'other side de Barbour plantation long side of our'n. Miss Nancy's been down to Richmond an' since I been gone she don't hab nobody to wait on her, an' so she tuk dis boy an' fixed him up in dese Richmond clothes. He says he's free. *Free,* mind ye! Dat's what all dese no count niggers is. But I'm watchin' him, an' de fust time he plays any o' dese yer free tricks on me he'll land in a spell o' sickness," and Chad choked himself with another chuckle.

The door swung back.

"Miss Caarter say dat she'll be down in a minute," said the scrap.

Chad straightened his face and brought it down to a semblance of austerity; always a difficult task with Chad.

"Who did you say was yere?" he asked.

"I didn't say—I handed her de kerd."

"How did you carry it?"

"In my pan."

COLONEL CARTER'S CHRISTMAS

"What did ye do wid de pan?"

The boy's face fell.

"I lef' it in de hall, sah."

"Sah! sah! Don't you 'sah' me. Ain't nobody 'sah' round yere but de Colonel. What I tell you to call me?"

"Uncle Chad."

"Dat's it, Uncle Chad. Now go 'long, honey, an' take yo' seat outside wid yo' pan; plenty folks comin', now dey know de Mist'iss here. Dar she is now. Dat's her step, on de stairs, Major. I doan' want her to catch me lookin' like dis. Drap into de kitchen, Major, as ye go out, I got sumpin' to show ye. Dem tarr'pins de Mist'iss fotch wid her make yo' mouf water."

Some women, when they enter a room, burst in like a child just out of school and overwhelm you with the joyousness of their greetings; others come in without a sound, settle into a seat and regale you in monotones with histories of either the attendant misery or the expected calamity.

Aunt Nancy floated in like a bubble blown along a carpet, bringing with her a radiance, a charm, a gentleness, a graciousness of welcome, a gladness at seeing you, so sincere and so heartfelt, that I always felt as if a window had been opened letting in the sunshine and the perfume of flowers.

"Oh, my dear Major!" and she held out her hand; that tiny little hand which lace becomes so well, and that always suggests its morning baptism of rose water.

Such a dainty white hand! I always bend over and kiss it whenever I have the chance, trying my best to be the gallant I know she would like me to be.

After the little ceremony of my salutation was over I handed her to a seat, still holding her finger-tips, bowing low just as her own cavaliers used to do in the days when she had half the County at her feet. I love these make-believe ceremonies when I am with her— and then again I truly think she would not be so happy without them. This over I took my place opposite so I could watch her face and the smiles playing across it —that face which the Colonel always said reminded him of "Summer roses a-bloom in October."

We talked of her journey and of how she had stood the cold and how reluctant she had been at first to leave Carter Hall, especially at the Christmas season, and of the Colonel (not a word, of course, about the encounter with Klutchem—no one would have dared breathe a word of that to her), and then of the scrap of a pickaninny she had brought with her.

"Isn't he too amusing? I brought him up as much to help dear Chad as for any other reason. But he is incorrigible at times and I fear I shall have to send him back to his mother. I thought the livery might increase his self-respect, but it only seems to have turned his head. He doesn't obey me at all, and is *so* forgetful. Chad is the only one of whom, I think, he is at all afraid."

A knock now sounded in the hall and I could hear the shuffling of Jim's feet, and the swinging back of

COLONEL CARTER'S CHRISTMAS

the door. Then Fitz's card was brought in—not on the silver tray this time, but clutched in the monkey paw of the pickaninny.

Aunt Nancy looked at him with a certain well-assumed surprise and drew back from the proffered card.

"James, is that the way to bring me a card? Have I not told you often——"

The boy looked at her, his face in a tangle of emotions. "De *Pan!* Fo' Gord, Mist'iss, I done forgot dat pan," and with a spring he was out again, returning with Fitz's pasteboard on the silver tray, closely followed by that gentleman himself, who was shaking with laughter over the incident.

"One of your body-guard, Aunt Nancy?" said Fitz, as he bent over and kissed her hand. It was astonishing how easily Fitz fell into these same old-time customs when he was with the dear lady—he, of all men.

"No, dear friend, one of the new race of whom I am trying to make a good servant. His grandmother in slave times belonged to a neighbor of ours, and this little fellow is the youngest of six. I've just been telling the Major what a trial he is to me. And now let me look at you. Ah! you have been working too hard. I see it in your eyes. Haven't you had some dreadful strain lately?"

Fitz declared on his honor, with one hand over his upper watch pocket, and the other still in hers, that he never felt better in his life, and that so idle had he become lately, that it was hard work for him to keep employed. And then Aunt Nancy made him sit beside her on the haircloth sofa, the one on which Fitz would not permit the Colonel to sleep, and I, being nearest, tucked a cushion under her absurdly small feet and rearranged about her shoulders her Indian mull shawl, which didn't require any rearranging at all. And after Fitz had told the dear lady for the third time how glad he was to see her, and after she had told him how glad she was to see both of us, and how she hoped dear George would soon secure the money necessary to build his railroad, so that we could all come to Carter Hall for next Christmas, she adding gravely that she really couldn't see any need for the road's existence or any hope of its completion, although she never said so to dear George, she being a woman and not expected to know much of such things; —after, I say, all these delightful speeches and attentions and confidences had been indulged in, Aunt Nancy bent her head, turned her sweet face framed in the lace cap and ribbons, first towards me and then back to Fitz again— she had been talking to Fitz all this time, I listening— and said with the air of a fairy godmother entertaining two children:

"And now I've got a great Christmas surprise for both of you, and you shall have one guess apiece as to what it is."

Fitz, with the memories of a former Christmas at Carter Hall still fresh in mind, and knowing the dear lady's generosity, and having seen the biggest bundle of feathers and the longest pair of legs he had ever laid his eyes on hanging head down on the measly wall

COLONEL CARTER'S CHRISTMAS

of the shabby yard as he entered, screwed up his eyes, cudgelled his brain by tapping his forehead with his forefinger, and blurted out:

"Wild turkey stuffed with chestnuts."

Aunt Nancy laughed until her side curls shook.

"Oh, you dreadful gourmand! Not a *bit* like a turkey. How mortified you will be when you find out! Go and stand in the corner, sir, with your face to the wall. Now, Major, it's your turn."

Fitz began to protest that he ought to have another chance, and that it had slipped out before he knew it, since he had never forgotten a brother of that same bird, one that he had eaten at her own table; but the little lady wouldn't hear another syllable, and waved him away with great dignity, whereupon Fitz buried his fat face in his hands, and said that life was really not worth the living, and that if anybody would suggest a comfortable way of committing suicide he would adopt it at once.

When my turn came, I, remembering the buttons on "Jeems," guessed a livery for Chad, at which the dear lady laughed more merrily than before, and Fitz remarked in a disgusted tone that the dense stupidity of some men was one of the characteristics of the time.

"No; it's nothing to eat and it's nothing to wear. It's a most charming young lady who at my earnest solicitation has consented to dine with us, and to whom I want you two young gentlemen (Fitz is forty if he's a day, and looks it) to be most devoted."

COLONEL CARTER'S CHRISTMAS

"Pretty?" asked Fitz, pulling up his collar—prinking in mock vanity.

"Yes, and better than pretty."

"Young?" persisted Fitz.

"Young, and most entertaining."

"Now listen both of you and I will tell you all about it. She lives up in one of your most desolate streets, Lafayette Place, I think, they call it, and in such a sombre house that it looks as if the windows had never been opened. Her mother is dead, and such a faded, hopeless-looking woman takes care of the house, a relation of the father's, I understand, who is a business friend of George's, and with whom he tells me he once had a slight misunderstanding. George did not want Christmas to pass with these differences unsettled, and so, of course, I went to call the very day I arrived and invited her and her father to dine with us on Christmas Eve. We always celebrate our Christmas then as you both know, on account of our old custom of giving Christmas day to our servants. And I am *so* glad I went. I did not, of course, see the father. Oh, it would make your heart ache to see the inside of that house. Everything costly and solid, and yet everything so joyless. I always feel sorry for such homes,— no flowers about, no books that are not locked up, no knick-knacks nor pretty things. I hope you will both help me to make her Christmas Eve a happy one. You perhaps may know her father, Mr. Fitzpatrick, —he is in Wall Street I hear, and his name is Klutchem."

COLONEL CARTER'S CHRISTMAS

Fitz, in his astonishment, so far forgot himself as to indulge in a low whistle.

"Then you *do* know him?"

"Oh, very well."

"And you tell me that Mr. Klutchem is really coming to dinner and going to bring his daughter?" asked Fitz, in a tone that made his surprise all the more marked.

"Yes; George had a note from him this morning saying his daughter would be here before dark and he would come direct from his office and meet her here in time for dinner. Isn't it delightful? You will be quite charmed with our guest, I'm sure. And about the father—tell me something of him?" Aunt Nancy inquired in her sweetest voice.

"About Mr. Klutchem? Well! Yes, to be sure. Why, Klutchem! Yes, of course. A most genial and kindly man," answered Fitz, controlling himself; "a little eccentric at times I have heard, but not more so than most men of his class. Not a man of much taste, perhaps, but most generous. Would give you anything in the world he didn't want, and be so delighted when you took it off his hands. Insisted on giving me a lot of stock the other day, but of course I wouldn't take it." This was said with so grave a face that its point escaped the dear lady.

"How very kind of him. Perhaps that is where his daughter gets her charm," replied Aunt Nancy, with a winning smile.

There is no telling what additional mendacities regarding the Klutchem family Fitz, who had now regained his equilibrium, would have indulged in, had I not knit my eyebrows at him behind Aunt Nancy's back as a warning to the mendacitor not to mislead the dear lady, whose disappointment, I knew, would only be the greater when she met Klutchem face to face.

When I had risen to take my leave Fitz excused himself for a moment and followed me into the hall.

"Klutchem coming to dinner, Major, and going to bring his daughter? What the devil do you think is up? If the Colonel wasn't so useless financially I'd think Klutchem had some game up his sleeve. But if that is so, why bring his daughter? My lawyer told me to-day the assault and battery case is all settled, so it can't be that. Wonder if the Colonel has converted Klutchem as to the proper way of running a bank? No, that's nonsense! Klutchem would skin a flea and sell the tallow, no matter what the Colonel said to him. Coming to dinner! Well, that gets me!"

As I shut the front door behind me and stopped for a minute on the top step overlooking the yard, I caught sight of the grocer emerging from the tunnel with a basket on his arm for Chad, who was standing below me outside his kitchen door with the half-picked duck in his hand. The settlement of "Misser Grocerman's" unpaid accounts by Miss Nancy on one of her former visits to Bedford Place had worked a double miracle—Chad no longer feared the dispenser of fine wines and other comforts, and the dispenser himself would have emptied his whole shop into Chad's kitchen and waited months for his pay had that loyal old servant permitted it. This was evident from the way in which Chad dropped the half-picked duck on a bench beside the door and hurried forward to help unpack the basket; and the deferential smile on the grocer's face as he took out one parcel after another, commenting on their quality and cheapness.

I had promised Chad to stop long enough to inspect Miss Nancy's "tarr' pins," and so I waited until Chad's duties were over.

"That's the cheekiest little coon ever come into the store," I hear the grocer say with a laugh. "I'd a-slid him out on his ear if he'd said much more."

Chad looked over his pile of bundles—they lay up on his arm; the top one held in place by his chin—and asked with some anxiety:

"Who, Jim? What did he do?"

"Do! He waltzed in yesterday afternoon with his head up and his under lip sticking out as if he owned the place. When I told him to take the sugar back with him, he said he wasn't carrying no bundles for nobody, he was waiting on Miss Carter. He's out at the gate now."

"Do ye hear dat, Major? Ain't dat 'nough to make a body sick? I been 'spectin' dis ever since he come. I'm gwinter stop dis foolishness short off."

The old darky waited until the grocer had reached the street, then he shouted into the gloom of the narrow passage:

"Here, Jim. Come here."

The scrap in buttons slammed to the wicket gate and came running through the tunnel.

"What you tell dat gemman yisterday when I sont you for dat sugar, wid yo' lip stickin' out big 'nough for a body ter sit on?"

The boy hung his head.

"You'se waitin' on Miss Caarter, is ye, an' ye ain't caarryin' no bundles? If I ever hear ye sass anybody round here agin, white or black, I'll tear dem buttons off ye an' skin ye alive—you'se caarryin' what I send ye for—do ye hear dat? *Free*, is ye? You'se free wid yo' sass an' dat's all de freedom you got."

"I—didn't know—yer want me ter—caa'ry it back," said the boy in a humble tone, but with the twinkle of a smouldering coal in his eye.

"Ye didn't? Who did ye think was gwine to caa'ry it back for ye? Maybe it was de Colonel or de Mist'iss or *me?*" Chad's voice had now risen to a high pitch, and with a touch of sarcasm in it which was biting. "Pretty soon you'll 'spec' somebody gwine to call for ye in dere caa'ridge. Yo' idea o' freedom is to wait on nobody and hab no manners. What ye got in yo' hand?"

"Cigarette white boy gimme,"—and the boy dropped the burning end on the brick pavement of the yard.

"Dat's mo' freedom, an' dat's all dis po' white trash is gwine to do for ye—stuffin' yo' head wid lies, an' yo' mouf wid a wad o' nastiness. Now go 'long an' git yo' pan."

COLONEL CARTER'S CHRISTMAS

Chad waited until the boy had mounted the steps and entered the house, then he turned to me.

"Po' li'l chin'ka'pin—he don't know no better. How's he gwine to git a bringin' up? Miss Nancy tryin' to teach him, but she ain't gwine make nuffin' of him. He's got pizened by dis freedom talk, an' he ain't gwine to git cured. Fust thing ye know he'll begin to think he's good as white folks, an' when he's got dat in his head he's done for. I'm gwine to speak to de Mist'iss 'bout dat boy, an' see if sumpin can't be done to save him fo' it gits too late; ain't nuffin' gwine to do him no good but a barr'l stave—hear dat—a barr'l stave!"

The Colonel had come in quietly and stood listening. I had heard the click of the outer gate, but supposed it was the grocer returning with the additional supplies.

"Who's Chad goin' to thresh, Major?" the Colonel asked, with a smile as he put his arm over my shoulder.

"Miss Nancy's pickaninny," I answered.

"What, little Jim?" There was a tone of surprise now in the Colonel's voice.

Chad stood abashed for a moment. He had stowed away the groceries, and had the duck in his hand again, his fingers fumbling among its feathers.

"'Scuse me, Colonel, I ain't gwine whale him, of co'se, 'thout yo' permission, but he's dat puffed up he'll bust fo' long."

"What's he been up to?"

"Sassin' Misser Grocerman—runnin' to de gate wid his head out like a tar'pin's, smoking dese yer paper seegars dat smell de whole place up vill'nous, 'stid of waitin' on de Mist'iss."

"And you think beatin' him will do him any good, Chad? How many times did yo' Marster John beat you?"

Chad looked up, and a smile broke over his face.

"I don't reckellmember airy lick de Marster ever laid on me."

"Raised you pretty well, didn't he, Chad?"

"Yas, sah—dat he did."

"Anybody beat you since you grew up?"

"No, sah."

"Pretty good, Chad, ain't you?"

"I try to be, sah."

"Well, now, be a little patient with that boy. It isn't his fault that he's sp'ilt; it's part of the damnable system this Gov'ment has put upon us since the war. Am I right, Major?"

I nodded assent.

Chad pulled out a handful of feathers from the duck, dropped them into a barrel near where we stood in the yard, and said, as if his mind was finally made up:

"Co'se, Colonel, I ain't nuffin' to say jes' 'cept dis. When I was dat boy's age I was runnin' 'round barefoot an' putty nigh naked, my shirt out o' my pants haalf de time; but Marse John tuk care o' me, an' when I got hongry I knowed whar dey was sumpin to eat an' I got it. Dat boy ain't had nobody take care o' him till de Mist'iss tuk him, and haalf de time he went hongry; no manners, no bringin' up—runnin'

COLONEL CARTER'S CHRISTMAS

wid po' white trash, gittin' his head full o' fool notions 'stid o' waitin' on his betters. Now look at him. Come in yere yisterday mornin', an' want borry my bresh to black his shoes. Den he must bresh his clothes wid yo' bresh—*yo*' bresh, mind you! I cotched him at it. Den he gits on his toes an' squints at hisself in de Mist'iss glass—I cotched him at dat, too—an' he ugly as one o' dem black tree-toads. You know what done dat? Dem Richmond clothes he's got on. I tell ye, Colonel, sumpin gotter be done, or dem buttons'll spile dat chile."

The Colonel laughed heartily.

"What does Miss Nancy say about yo' barr'l stave?"

"She don't say nuffin', 'cause she don't know."

"Well, don't you thresh Jim till you see her."

"No, sah."

"And Chad?"

"Yes, sah."

"When you do, pick out a little stave. Come, Major, go back with me for just ten minutes mo' and see the dea'est woman in the world."

V

The day before Christmas was a never-to-be-forgotten day in Bedford Place. Great preparations were being made for the event of the evening, and everybody helped.

Little Jim under the tutelage of Chad, and in hourly fear of the promised thrashing—it had never gone beyond the promise since the Colonel's talk—had so far forgotten his clothes and his dignity as to load himself with Christmas greens—one long string wound around his body like a boa constrictor—much to the amusement of the Colonel, who was looking out of the dining-room window when he emerged from the tunnel. Aunt Nancy went all the way to the grocery for some big jars for the flowers I had sent her (not to mention a bunch of roses of the Colonel's) and brought one of the pots back in her own hand; and spoke in so low and gentle a voice when she purchased them that everybody in the place ceased talking to listen.

The Colonel busied himself drawing, in the most careful and elaborate manner, the wax-topped corks of certain be-cobwebbed bottles that had been delivered the night before by no less a person than Duncan's own agent, and to one of which was attached

COLONEL CARTER'S CHRISTMAS

Fitz's visiting card bearing his compliments and best wishes. The contents of these crusted bottles the Colonel had duly emptied into two cut-glass decanters with big stoppers—heirlooms from Carter Hall—placing the decanters themselves in two silver coasters bearing the Coat-of-Arms of his family, and the whole combination on the old-fashioned sideboard which graced the wall opposite the fireplace. Chad, with the aid of the grocer, had produced as assistant below stairs, from a side street behind Jefferson Market, a saddle-colored female who wore flowers in her hat, and who, to his infinite amusement, called him "Mister."

"Can't do nothin' big, Major, dis place's so mighty small," he called to me from his kitchen door as I mounted the yard steps, "but it's gwine to smell mighty good round here 'bout dinner-time.

Under the deft touches of all these willing hands it is not to be wondered at that the Colonel's cosy rooms developed a quality unknown to them before, delightful as they had always been: The table boasted an extra leaf (an extra leaf was always ready for use in every dining-room of the Colonel's); the candlesticks, old family plate and andirons, dulled by the winter's use, shone with phenomenal brightness; the mantel supported not only half a dozen bottles of claret (Duncan's cellars, Fitz's selection) but a heap of roses that reached as high as the clock, while over the door, around the windows and high up over the two fireplaces—everywhere, in fact, where a convenient nail or hook could be found—were entwined in loops and circles, the Christmas greens and holly berries that little Jim had staggered under.

The crowning sensation of the coming event stood in the corner of the rear room,—a small Christmas tree grown in the woods behind Carter Hall. A little tree with all its branches perfect; large enough to hold its complement of candles; small enough to stand in the centre of the table within reach of everybody's hand. Aunt Nancy had picked it out herself. She must always respect the sentiment. No bought tree would do for her on such an occasion. It must be to the manor born, nourished in her own soil, warmed by the same sun and watered by the same rains. The bringing of a tree from her own home at Carter Hall to cheer the Colonel's temporary resting-place in Bedford Place, was to her like the bringing of a live coal from old and much loved embers with which to start a fire on a new hearth.

These several preparations complete—and it was quite late in the day when they were complete (in the twilight really)—Chad threw a heap of wood beside the fireplace, brushed the hearth of its ashes, laid a pile of India Blue plates in front of its cheery blaze (no crime, the Colonel often said, was equal to putting a hot duck on a cold plate), placed the Colonel's chair in position, arranged a cushion in Aunt Nancy's empty rocker; gave a few finishing touches to the table; stopped a moment in the kitchen below to give some instructions to the saddle-colored female as to the length of time a

COLONEL CARTER'S CHRISTMAS

canvas-back should remain in the oven, and stepped back into his little room, there to array himself in white jacket and gloves, the latter tucked into his outside pocket ready for instant use.

During these final preparations the Colonel was upstairs donning a costume befitting the occasion—snow-white waistcoat, white scarf and patent-leather pumps, with little bows over the toes, limp as a poodle's ears, and his time-honored coat, worn wide open of course, the occasion being one of great joyousness and good cheer. These necessities of toilet over, the Colonel descended the narrow staircase, threw wide the dining-room door, shook me cordially by the hand with the manner of a man welcoming a distinguished guest whom he had not seen for years (I had just arrived); bowed to Chad as if he had been one of a long line of servants awaiting the coming of their lord (festive occasions always produced this frame of mind in the Colonel); laid a single white rose beside the plates of his two lady guests—one for Miss Carter and the other for Miss Klutchem—and glancing around the apartment expressed his admiration of all that had been done. Then he settled himself in his easy chair, with his feet on the fender, and spread his moist, newly-washed hands to the blaze.

Aunt Nancy now entered in a steel-gray silk and new cap and ribbons, her delicate, frail shoulders covered by a light scarf, little Jim following behind her with her ball of yarn and needles, and a low stool for her feet. The only change in Jim was a straggly groove down the middle of his wool, where he had attempted a "part" like Chad's.

"I'm glad Mr. Klutchem is comin', Nancy," said the Colonel when the dear lady had taken her seat with Jim behind her chair. "From what you tell me of his home I'm afraid that he must pass a great many lonely hours. And then again I cannot forget his generosity to a friend of mine once in his hour of trial."

"What was the trouble between you and Mr. Klutchem, George?" she asked in reply, spreading out her skirts and taking the knitting from Jim's hands.

The Colonel hesitated and for a moment did not answer. Aunt Nancy raised her eyes to his and waited.

"I diffe'ed from him on the value of some secu'ities, Nancy, and for a time the argument became quite heated."

"And it left some ill-feeling?"

"Oh, no; on the contrary, it seemed to open a way for an important settlement in a friend's affairs which may have the best and most lastin' results. I believe I am quite within the mark, Major, when I make that statement," added the Colonel, turning to me.

"No doubt of it, Colonel," I answered. "That same friend told me that he hadn't enjoyed anything so much for years as Mr. Klutchem's visit to his office that morning."

"Well, I am so glad," said Aunt Nancy—"so glad!" The "friend's" name had been too obviously concealed by both the Colonel and myself for her to press any inquiries in that direction. "And you have not seen the daughter?" She continued.

"No, Mr. Klutchem was ill at a friend's house when I called on him once befo', and his family were not in the room. I shall have that pleasure for the first time when she arrives."

Chad now entered, bowed low to his Mistress, his invariable custom, and began to light the candles on the mantelpiece and sideboard, and then those in the two big silver candlesticks which decorated each end of the table, with its covers for six. Little Jim still stood behind his Miss Nancy's chair: he was not to be trusted with any of Chad's important duties.

There came a knock at the door.

"That's dear Fitz," said the Colonel. "He promised to come early."

Chad looked meaningly at the scrap, and little Jim, in answer to the sound of Fitz's knuckles, left the room, picking up his "pan" from the hall table as he answered the summons.

At this moment the dear lady dropped her ball of yarn, and the Colonel and I stooped down to recover it. This was a duty from which even Chad was relieved when either of us was present. While we were both on our knees groping around the legs of the sideboard, the door opened softly, and a sweet, low voice said:

"Please, I'm Katy Klutchem, and I've come to the Christmas tree."

The Colonel twisted his head quickly.

COLONEL CARTER'S CHRISTMAS

A little girl of six or eight, her chubby cheeks aglow with the cold of the winter twilight, a mass of brown curls escaping from her hat framing a pretty face, stood looking at him—he was still on his knees—with wide, wondering eyes. He had expected to welcome a young woman of twenty, he told me afterwards, not a child. Aunt Nancy inadvertently, perhaps, or because she supposed he knew, had omitted any reference to her age. I, too, had fallen into the same error.

The dear lady without rising from her seat held out her two hands joyously:

"Oh, you darling little thing! Come here until I take off your hat and coat."

The Colonel had now risen to his feet, the ball of yarn in his hand, his eyes still on the apparition. No child had ever stepped foot inside the cosy quarters since his occupation. Katy returned his gaze with that steadfast, searching look common to some children, summing up by intuition the dangers and the man. Then, with her face breaking into a smile at the Colonel, she started towards Aunt Nancy.

But the Colonel had come to his senses now.

"So you are not a grown-up lady at all," he cried, with a joyous note in his voice, as he advanced towards her, "but just a dear little girl."

"Why, did you think I was grown-up? I'm only seven. Oh, what a nice room, and is the Christmas tree here?"

"It is not lighted yet, dearie," replied Aunt Nancy, her fingers busy with the top button of the child's cloak, the eager, expectant face twisted around as if she was looking for something. "It's over there in the corner."

"Let me show it to you," said the Colonel, and he took her hand. "Major, please bring one of the candles."

The child's eyes sought the Colonel's face. The first look she had given him as she entered the room had settled all doubt in her mind; children know at a glance whom they can trust.

"Please do," she answered simply, and her grasp closed over his. The cloak and hat were off now, and Jim was bearing them upstairs to be laid on Miss Nancy's bed.

As the small, frail hand touched his own I saw a strange look come into the Colonel's eyes. It was evidently all he could do to keep from stooping down and kissing her.

Instinctively my mind went back to a night not long before when I had found him sitting by his fire. "There is but one thing in all the world, Major," he said to me then, "sweeter than the song of a robin in the spring, and that is the laughter of a child."

I knew therefore, as I looked at these two, what the little hand that lay in his meant to him.

So I held the candle and the Colonel lighted the tip end of just one tiny taper to show her how it burned, and what a pretty light it made shining through the green; and Katy clapped her hands and said it was beautiful, and such a darling little tree, and not at all like the big one in the Sunday School that reached nearly to the ceiling, and that nobody dared to touch. And then we all went back to the fire and the Colonel's chair, and before I knew it he had her by his side with his arm around her shoulders, telling her stories, while Aunt Nancy and Jim and I sat listening.

And so absorbed was he in the new life, and so happy with the child, that he only gave Fitz three fingers to shake when that friend of his heart came in, and never once said he was glad to see him—an unprecedented omission—and never once made the slightest allusion to the expected guest of the evening, Mr. Klutchem, now that his daughter had turned out to be a child of seven instead of a full-grown woman of twenty.

The Colonel told her of the great woods behind Carter Hall, where the Christmas tree had grown, and the fox with the white tail that lived there, and that used to pop into his hole in the snow, and how you'd pass right by and never see him because his tail, which was the biggest part of him, was so white; and the woodpeckers that bored into the bark with their long, sharp bills; and finally of the big turkeys that strutted and puffed their feathers and spread their tails about and ran so fast nothing could catch them.

"Not even a dog?" interrupted the child. She had crawled up into his arms now and was looking up into his face with wondering eyes.

"Dogs!" answered the Colonel contemptuously, "why, these turkeys would be up and gone befo' a dog could turn 'round."

COLONEL CARTER'S CHRISTMAS

"Tell me what they are like. Have they long—long legs—so?" and she stretched out her arms.

"Oh, longer—terrible long legs—long as *this*"—and the Colonel's arms went out to their full length.

Jim's eyes were now popping out of his head, but his place was behind his Mistress's chair, ready for her orders, and he had had so many scoldings that day that he thought it best not to move.

"And does he puff himself out like a real turkey in the picture books?"

"Oh, worse than a real turkey,—big as *so*"—and the Colonel's arms went round in a circle.

The child thought hard for a moment until she had the picture of the strutting gobbler fastened in her mind, and said, cuddling closer to the Colonel: "Tell me some more."

"About turkeys?"

"Yes, about turkeys."

"About wild ones or tame ones?"

"Was that a wild one that the dogs couldn't catch?"

"Yes."

"Then tell me about some tame ones. Do they live in the woods?"

"No, they live in the barnyard with the chickens, and the cows, and the horses. Why, did you never see one?"

"Yes, but I want to hear you tell about them—that's better than seeing."

Jim could hold in no longer. He had become so

excited that he kept rubbing one shoe against the other, twisting and squirming like an eel. At last he burst out:

"An' one o' gobble-gobble was dat ornery, Mammy Henny shut him up in de coop!"

Aunt Nancy turned in astonishment, and Chad, who had come in with some dishes, was about to crush him with a look, when the Colonel said, with a sly twinkle in his eye:

"What did he do, Jim?"

"Jes' trompled de li'l teeny chickens an' eat up all de corn an' wouldn't let nobody come nigh him. An' he was dat swelled up!"

Katy laughed, and turning to the Colonel, said:

"Tell me about that one."

The Colonel ruminated for a moment, looked at Chad with a half-humorous expression, and motioned to little Jim to come over and stand by his chair so that he could hear the better, his own arm still about Katy, her head on his shoulder.

"About that big gobbler, Katy, that was so bad they had to put him in a coop?"

"Yes, that very one."

"Well, when I fust knew him he was a little teeny turkey—oh, not near so high as Jim; 'bout up to Jim's knees, I reckon. He'd follow 'round after his mammy and go where she wanted him to go and mind her like a nice little turkey as he was. He didn't live on my plantation then—he lived on Judge Barbour's plantation next to mine. Well, one day, Aunt Nancy

COLONEL CARTER'S CHRISTMAS

—that dear lady over there—wanted a fine young turkey, and this little knee-high turkey was growin' to be a big turkey, and so she brought him over and gave him the run of the barnyard.

"She was just as good to him as she could be. She made a nice clean place for him to live in, so his feathers wouldn't get dirty any mo', and he didn't have to run 'round lookin' for grasshoppers and beetles and little worms as he did at home, but he had a nice bowl of mush eve'y day and a place to go to sleep in all by himself, and Aunt Nancy did everythin' she could to make him comfo'table.

"Well, what do you think happened? Just as soon as that turkey found out he was bein' taken caare of better than the hens and the roosters and all the other little turkeys he had left at home, he began to put on airs. He breshed his feathers out and he strutted around same as if he owned the whole barnyard, and he'd go down to the pond and look at himself in the water; and he got so proud that whenever old Mrs. Hen or old Mr. Rooster would say 'Good-mornin'' to him as kind and as nice as could be, he wouldn't answer politely, but he'd stick up his head and go 'Gobble-gobble-gobble!' and then he'd swell up again and puff out his chest and march himself off. Pretty soon he got so sassy that nobody could live with him. Why, he didn't care what he did and who he stepped on. He trampled on two po' little chicks one day that were just out of the shell and mashed them flat and did all sorts of dreadful things."

"What an awful turkey! Poor little chickens," sighed Katy. "Go on."

"Next thing he did was to steal off and smoke cigarettes."

Katy raised her head and looked up into the Colonel's eyes.

"Why, turkeys can't smoke, can they?"

"Oh, no—of co'se not—I forgot. That's another story and I got them mixed up. Where was I? Oh, yes, when he got so sassy."

Katy dropped her head on his shoulder again. Jim was now listening with all his might, his only fear being that Chad or Miss Nancy or the knocker on the front door would summon him before the story was ended.

"Well," continued the Colonel, "that went on and on and on till there wasn't any livin' with him. Even dear Aunt Nancy couldn't get along with him, which is a dreadful thing to say of anybody. So one day"—here the Colonel's voice dropped to a tone of grave importance—"one day—Mammy Henny—that's the wife of Chad over there by the table, crep' up behind this wicked, sassy little turkey, when he was swellin' around so big he couldn't see his feet, and she grabbed him by the neck and two legs, and befo' he knew where he was, plump he went into a big coop, and the door was shut tight. He hollered and squawked and flapped his wings terrible, but that didn't make any diff'ence; in he went and there he stayed. He pushed with his long legs, and stuck his head out through the

COLONEL CARTER'S CHRISTMAS

slats, and did all he could to get out, but it was no use. Next day Mammy Henny got a great big knife—oh, an awful long knife——"

"How long?" asked the child.

"Oh, a dreadful long knife—'most as long as Jim, here"—and the Colonel laid his hand on the boy's shoulder—"and she sharpened it on a big grindstone, and Mammy Henny put some corn in the little trough outside the slats, and when this bad, wicked turkey poked his head out—WHACK—went the knife, and off went his head, and he was dead—dead—dead!"

As the solemn words fell from his lips, the Colonel broke into a laugh, and in a burst of tenderness threw his arms around the child and kissed her as if he would like to eat her up.

Katy was clapping her hands now.

"Oh, I'm just *too* glad. And the poor little chickies —served him just right. I was afraid he'd get out and run away."

The Colonel stole a look at Jim. The scrap stood, looking into the fire, a wondering expression on his face. How much of the story was truth and how much fiction evidently puzzled Jim.

During the telling everybody in the room, Fitz, Miss Nancy—all of us, in fact,—had been watching Katy's delight and Jim's eager brown face, turned to the Colonel, the whites of his eyes big as saucers. Watching, too, the Colonel's impartial manner to both of his listeners—black and white alike—the only distinction being that the black boy stood, while the white child lay nestled in his arms.

Chad, as the story progressed, had crept up behind the Colonel's chair, where he could hear without being seen, and was listening as eagerly as if he were a boy again. He had often told me that his old master, the Colonel's father, used to tell him and the Colonel stories when they were boys together, but I had never seen the Colonel in the rôle before.

When the allusion to the cigarettes escaped the Colonel's lips a smile overspread Chad's visage, and a certain triumphant look crept into his eyes. With the child's laughter still ringing through the room, Chad tapped Jim on the arm, led him to one side, held his lean, wrinkled finger within an inch of the boy's nose and said in a sepulchral tone:

"Did ye hear dat? Do ye know who dat sassy, low-lived, mizzable, no-count, ornery turkey was, dat kep' a-swellin' up, thinkin' he was *free* an' somebody great till dat caarvin' knife tuk his head off? Dat's *you!*"

In the midst of this scene, Katy still in the Colonel's arms, Aunt Nancy knitting quietly, talking to Fitz in an undertone, and I forming part of the circle around the fire, watching the Colonel's delight and joy over his new guest—the dining-room door was pushed open, and Mr. Klutchem stepped in.

"I found the outside door ajar, Colonel," he blurted out, "and heard you all laughing, and so I just walked in. Been here long, Katy?"

COLONEL CARTER'S CHRISTMAS

For an instant I was sorry he had come; it was like the dropping of a stone into a still pool.

The child slid out from the Colonel's lap, with an expression on her face as if she had been caught in some act she should be ashamed of, and stood close to the Colonel's chair, as if for protection. Aunt Nancy, Fitz, and I rose to our feet to welcome the newcomer. The Colonel, having to pull himself out from the depths of his chair, was the last to rise. He had been so absorbed in the child that he had entirely forgotten both the father and the dinner. It, however, never took the Colonel long to recover his equilibrium where a matter of courtesy was concerned.

"My dear, Mr. Klutchem," he cried, throwing out his chest, and extending his hand graciously. "This is, indeed, a pleasure. Permit me to present you to my aunt, Miss Caarter, of Virginia, who has left her home to gladden our Christmas with her presence. The gentlemen, of co'se, you already know. Yo' little daughter, suh, is a perfect sunbeam. She has so crept into our hearts that we feel as if we never wanted her to leave us——" and he laid his hand on the child's head.

The banker shook hands with Aunt Nancy, remarked that he was sorry he had not been at home when she called, extended the same five fingers to me, and again in turn to Fitz, and sat down on the edge of a chair which Jim had dragged up for him. Katy walked over and stood by her father's knee. Her holiday seemed over.

COLONEL CARTER'S CHRISTMAS

"Rather sharp weather, isn't it?" Mr. Klutchem began, rubbing his hands and looking about him. He had not forgotten the cheeriness of the rooms the day of his first visit; in their holiday attire they were even more delightful. "I suppose, Colonel, you don't have such weather in your State," he continued.

The Colonel, who was waiting for a cue—any cue served the Colonel, weather, politics, finance, everything but morals and gossip, these he never discussed, launched out in his inimitable way describing the varied kinds of weather indigenous to his part of the State: the late spring frosts with consequent damage to the peach crop; the heat of summer; the ice storms and the heavy falls of soft snow that were gone by midday; the banker describing in return the severities of the winters in Vermont, his own State, and the quality of the farming land which, he said, with a dry laugh, often raised four stone fences to the acre, and sometimes five.

Before the two had talked many minutes I saw to my delight that the waters of the deep pool which I feared had become permanently troubled by the sudden arrival of the broker, were assuming their former tranquil condition. Aunt Nancy resumed her knitting awaiting the time when Chad should announce dinner. Katy, finding that her father had no immediate use for her—not an unusual experience with Katy—moved off and stood by Aunt Nancy, watching the play of her needles, the dear lady talking to her in a low voice, while Fitz and I put our heads together, and

COLONEL CARTER'S CHRISTMAS

with eyes and ears open, followed with close attention the gradual thawing out of the hard ice of the practical man of affairs under the warm sun of the Colonel's hospitality.

Soon the long expected hour arrived, a fact made known first by the saddle-colored female to Jim standing at the head of the stairs, and who promptly conveyed it to Chad's ear in a whisper that was heard all over the room, and finally by Chad himself, who announced the welcome news to Miss Nancy with a flourish that would have done credit to the master of ceremonies at a Lord Mayor's banquet; drawing out a chair for her on the right of the Colonel, another on his left for Mr. Klutchem, and a third for Miss Klutchem, who was seated between Fitz and me. He then stationed Jim, now thoroughly humbled by the chastening he had received, at the door in the hall to keep open an unbroken line of communication between the fragrant kitchen below and the merry table above.

The seating of the guests brought the cosy circle together—and what a picture it was: The radiance of Aunt Nancy's face as she talked to one guest and another, twisting her head like a wren's to see Mr. Klutchem the better when the Colonel stood up to carve the ducks: and the benignant, patriarchal, bless-you-my-children smile that kept irradiating the Virginian's visage as, knife in hand, he descanted on the various edibles and drinkables that made his native County a rare place to be born in; and Mr. Klutchem's quiet, absorbed manner, so different from his boisterous outbreaks—a fact which astonished Fitz most of all; and Katy's unrestrained laughter breaking in at all times like a bird's, and Chad's beaming face and noiseless tread, taking the dishes from Jim's hands as carefully as an antiquary would so many curios, and placing them without a sound before his master—yes, all these things indeed made a picture that could never be forgotten.

As to the quality and toothsomeness of the several and various dishes—roast, broiled, and baked—that kept constantly arriving, there was, there could be, but one opinion:

Nobody had ever seen such oysters; nobody had ever eaten such terrapin! Nobody had ever tasted such ducks!—so Mr. Klutchem said, and he ought to have known, for he had the run of the Clubs. Nobody had crunched such celery nor had revelled in such sweet potatoes; nor had anybody since the beginning of the world ever smacked their lips over such a ham.

"One of our razor-backs, Mr. Klutchem," said the Colonel; "fed on acorns, and so thin that he can jump through a palin' fence and never lose a hair. When a pig down our way gets so fat that a darky can catch him, we have no use for him"—and the Colonel laughed—a laugh which was echoed in a suppressed grin by Chad, the witticism not being intended for him.

Soon there stole over every one in the room that sense of peace and contentment which always comes

COLONEL CARTER'S CHRISTMAS

when one is at ease in an atmosphere where love and kindness reign. The soft light of the candles, the low, rich color of the simple room with its festoons of cedar and pine, the aroma of the rare wine, and especially the spicy smell of the hemlock warmed by the burning tapers—that rare, unmistakable smell which only Christmas greens give out and which few of us know but once a year, and often not then; all had their effect on host and guests. Katy became so happy that she lost all fear of her father and prattled on to Fitz and me (we had pinned to her frock the rose the Colonel had bought for the "grown-up daughter," and she was wearing it just as Aunt Nancy wore hers), and Aunt Nancy in her gentle voice talked finance to Mr. Klutchem in a way that made him open his eyes, and Fitz laughingly joined in, giving a wide berth to anything bearing on "corners" or "combinations" or "shorts" and "longs," while I, to spare Aunt Nancy, kept one eye on Jim, winking at him with it once or twice when he was about to commit some foolishness, and so the happy feast went on.

As to the Colonel, he was never in better form. To him the occasion was the revival of the old Days of Plenty—the days his soul coveted and loved: his to enjoy, his to dispense.

But if it had been delightful before, what was it when Chad, after certain mysterious movements in the next room, bore aloft the crowning glory of the evening, and placed it with all its candles in the centre of the table, the Colonel leaning far back in his chair to give him room, his coat thrown wide, his face aglow, his eyes sparkling with the laughter that always kept him young!

Then it was that the Colonel gathering under his hand the little sheaf of paper lamplighters which Chad had twisted, rose from his seat, picked up a slender glass that had once served his father ("only seben o' dat kind left," Chad told me) and which that faithful servitor had just filled from the flow of the old decanter of like period, and with a wave of his hand as if to command attention, said, in a clear, firm voice that indicated the dignity of the occasion:

"My friends,—my *vehy dear* friends, I should say, for I can omit none of you—certainly not this little angel who has captured our hearts, and surely not our distinguished guest, Mr. Klutchem, who has honored us with his presence—befo' I kindle with the torch of my love these little beacons which are to light each one of us on our way until another Christmas season overtakes us; befo', I say, these sparks burst into life, I want you to fill yo' glasses (Chad had done that to the brim—even little Katy's) and drink to the health and happiness of the lady on my right, whose presence is always a benediction and whose loyal affection is one of the sweetest treasures of my life!"

Everybody except the dear lady stood up—even little Katy—and Aunt Nancy's health was drunk amid her blushes, she remarking to Mr. Klutchem that George would always embarrass her with these too flattering speeches of his, which was literally true, this being the

COLONEL CARTER'S CHRISTMAS

fourth time I had heard similar sentiments expressed in the dear lady's honor.

This formal toast over, the Colonel's whole manner changed. He was no longer the dignified host conducting the feast with measured grace. With a spring in his voice and a certain unrestrained joyousness, he called to Chad to bring him a light for his first lamplighter. Then, with the paper wisp balanced in his hand, he began counting the several candles, peeping into the branches with the manner of a boy.

"One—two—three—fo'—yes, plenty of them, but we are goin' to begin with the top one. This is yours, Nancy—this little white one on the vehy tip-top. Gentlemen, this top candle is always reserved for Miss Caarter," and the lighted taper kindled it into a blaze. "Just like yo' eyes, my dear, burnin' steadily and warmin' everybody," and he tapped her hand caressingly with his fingers. "And now, where is that darlin' little Katy's—she must have a white one, too—here it is. Oh, what a brave little candle! Not a bit of sputterin' or smoke. See, dearie, what a beautiful blaze! May all your life be as bright and happy. And here is Mr. Klutchem's right alongside of Katy's—a fine red one. There he goes, steady and clear and strong. And Fitz—dear old Fitz. Let's see what kind of a candle Fitz should have. Do you know, Fitz, if I had my way, I'd light the whole tree for you. One candle is absurd for Fitz! There, Fitz, it's off—another red one! All you millionaires must have red candles! And the Major! Ah, the Major!"—and he held out his hand to me—"Let's see—yaller? No, that will never do for you, Major. Pink? That's better. There now, see how fine you look and how evenly you burn—just like yo' love, my dear boy, that never fails me."

The circle of the table was now complete; each guest had a candle alight, and each owner was studying the several wicks as if the future could be read in their blaze: Aunt Nancy with a certain seriousness. To her the custom was not new; the memories of her life were interwoven with many just such top candles,—one I knew of myself, that went out long, long ago, and has never been rekindled since.

The Colonel stopped, and for a moment we thought he was about to take his seat, although some wicks were still unlighted—his own among them.

Instantly a chorus of voices went up: "You have forgotten your own, Colonel—let me light this one for you," etc., etc. Even little Katy had noticed the omission, and was pulling at my sleeve to call attention to the fact: the Colonel's candle was the only one she really cared for.

"One minute—" cried the Colonel. "Time enough; the absent ones fust"—and he stooped down and peered among the branches—"yes,—that's just the very one. This candle, Mr. Klutchem, is for our old Mammy Henny, who is at Caarter Hall, carin' for my property, and who must be pretty lonely to-day—ah, there you go, Mammy!—blazin' away like one o' yo' own fires!"

Each guest had a candle alight.

COLONEL CARTER'S CHRISTMAS

Three candles now were all that were left unlighted; two of them side by side on the same branch, a brown one and a white one, and below these a yellow one standing all alone.

The Colonel selected a fresh taper, kindled it in the flame of Aunt Nancy's top candle, and turning to Chad, who was standing behind his chair, said:

"I'm goin' to put you, Chad, where you belong,—right alongside of me. Here, Katy darlin', take this taper and light this white candle for me, and I'll light the brown one for Chad," and he picked up another taper, lighted it, and handed it to the child.

"Now!"

As the two candles flashed into flame, the Colonel leaned over, and holding out his hand to the old servant—boys together, these two, said in a voice full of tenderness:

"Many years together, Chad,—many years, old man."

Chad's face broke into a smile as he pressed the Colonel's hand:

"Thank ye, marster," was all he trusted himself to say—a title the days of freedom had never robbed him of—and then he turned his head to hide the tears.

During this whole scene little Jim had stood on tiptoe, his eyes growing brighter and brighter as each candle flashed into a blaze. Up to the time of the lighting of the last guest candle his face had expressed nothing but increasing delight. When, however,

COLONEL CARTER'S CHRISTMAS

Mammy Henny's candle, and then Chad's were kindled, I saw an expression of wonderment cross his features which gradually settled into one of profound disappointment.

But the Colonel had not yet taken his seat. He had relighted the taper—this time from Mammy Henney's candle—and stood with it in his hand, peering into the branches as if looking for something he had lost.

"Ah, here's another. I wonder—who—this—little—yaller—candle—can—be—for," he said slowly, looking around the room and accentuating each word. "I reckon they're all here—Let me see—Aunt Nancy, Mr. Klutchem, Katy, Fitz, the Major, Mammy Henny, Chad, and me—Yes—all here—Oh!!" and he looked at the boy with a quizzical smile on his face—"I came vehy near forgettin.'

"This little yaller candle is Jim's."

. . . .

When it was all over; and Aunt Nancy herself had tied on Katy's hat and tucked the tippet into her neck, and buttoned her coat so that not a breath of cold air could get inside; and when Jim stood holding Mr. Klutchem's hat in the hall, with Chad but a few feet away; and when Mr. Klutchem had said good-by to Aunt Nancy, and had turned to take the extended hand of the Colonel, I heard the banker say, in a voice as if a tear had choked it:

"Carter, you're mighty good stuff and I like you. What you've taught me to-night I'll never forget.

COLONEL CARTER'S CHRISTMAS

Katy never had a mother, and I know now she's never had a home. Good-night."

"Come, Katy, I guess I'll carry you, little girl—" and he picked up the child, wound her reluctant arms about his neck, and went out into the night.

THE ROMANCE OF AN
OLD-FASHIONED GENTLEMAN

THE ROMANCE OF AN OLD-FASHIONED GENTLEMAN

I

Blossom week in Maryland! The air steeped in perfume and soft as a caress; the sky a luminous gray interwoven with threads of silver, flakings of pearl and tiny scales of opal.

All the hill-sides smothered in bloom—of peach, cherry, and pear; in waves, windrows and drifts of pink and ivory. Here and there, fluffy white, a single tree upheld like a bride's bouquet ready for my lady's hand when she goes to meet her lord. In the marshes flames of fringed azaleas and the tracings of budding birch and willow outspread like the sticks of fans. At their feet, shouldering their way upward, big dock leaves—vigorous, lusty leaves—eager to flaunt their verdure in the new awakening. Everywhere the joyous songs of busy birds fresh from the Southland—flying shuttles these, of black, blue and brown, weaving homes in the loom of branch and bud.

To the trained eye of young Adam Gregg, the painter, all this glory of blossom, hill-side, and pearly tinted sky came as a revelation and a delight. Drawing rein on his sorrel mare he raised himself in his stirrups and swept his glance over the landscape, feasting his eyes on the note of warmth in the bloom of the peach—a blossom unknown to his more northern clime, on the soft brown of the pastures, and on the filmy blue of the distant hills melting into the gray haze of the April morning. Suddenly a thrill shot through him and a fresh enthusiasm rose in his heart: with all this wealth of color about him, what would not his brush accomplish.

Swinging in his seat he readjusted the rain-cloak and painting-kit that were strapped to his saddle-bags, and rode on, his slouch hat pushed back from his forehead to cool his brow, his gray riding-coat unbuttoned and hanging loose, the brown riding-boots gripped about the mare's girth.

As he neared his destination the concluding lines of the letter of introduction tucked away in his pocket kept recurring to his mind. He was glad his subject was to be a woman—one near his own age. Women understood him better, and he them. It was the face and shoulders of a young and pretty woman—and a countess, too—which had won for him his first Honorable Mention in Munich. Would he be as lucky with the face and shoulders of the "beautiful girl-wife of Judge Colton"?

Soon the chimneys and big dormer-windows of Derwood Manor, surmounting the spacious colonial porch with its high pillars, rose above the skirting of trees. Then came the quaint gate with its brick posts topped by stone urns, through which swept a wide road bor-

OLD-FASHIONED GENTLEMAN

dered by lilac bushes   Dismounting at the horse-block the young painter handed the reins to a negro boy who had advanced to meet him, and, making his way through a group of pickaninnies and snuffing hounds, mounted the porch.

The Judge was waiting for him on the top step with both hands outstretched in welcome; a man of fifty, smooth-shaven, with iron-gray hair, a thin, straight mouth and a jaw as square as a law book.

"You needn't look for your letter, Mr. Gregg," he exclaimed heartily. "The nephew of my old classmate is always a welcome guest at Derwood Manor. We have been expecting you all the morning—" and the Judge shook the young man's hand as if he had known him from babyhood. It was in the early fifties and the hatreds of later years were unknown among men of equal social position in a land where hospitality was a religion. "Let me present you to Mrs. Colton and my little son, Phil."

Adam turned, and it seemed to him as if the glory of all the blossoms he had seen that day had gone into the making of a woman. Dressed all in white, a wide blue sash about her slender waist; graceful as a budding branch swaying in a summer wind; with eyes like rifts of blue seen through clouds of peach bloom; hair of spun gold in lifted waves about her head, one loosened curl straying over her beautiful shoulders; mouth and teeth a split pomegranate studded with seeds of pearl —she seemed the very embodiment of all the freshness, beauty, and charm of the awakening spring.

Instantly all the flesh tones from rose madder and cadmium to indigo-blue ran riot in his head. "What coloring," he kept saying to himself—"What a skin, and the hair and shoulders, and the curl that breaks the line of the throat—never was there such a woman!"

Even as he stood looking into her eyes, pretending to listen to her words of welcome, he was deciding on the colors he would use and the precise pose in which he would paint her.

"And it is such a delight to have you with us," she was saying in joyous tones, as though his coming brought a holiday. "When I knew you were to be here I began right away to build castles. You are to paint my portrait first, and then you are to paint Phil's. Isn't that it, Judge? Come Phil, dear, and shake hands with Mr. Gregg."

"Whichever you please," Adam replied simply, the little boy's hand in his. "I only hope I shall be able to do justice to you both. It will be my fault if I don't with all this beauty about me. I am really dazed by these wonderful fruit-trees."

"Yes, we're going to have a good season," exclaimed the Judge—"best we have had for years, peaches especially. We expect a——"

"Oh, I only meant the coloring," interrupted Gregg, his cheeks flushing. "It's wonderfully lovely."

"And you don't have spring blossoms North?" asked Mrs. Colton. Her own eyes had been drinking in the charm of his personality; no color-schemes or palette-tones were interesting her. The straight, lithe,

OLD-FASHIONED GENTLEMAN

figure, square shoulders, open, honest face, sunny brown eyes, with the short, crisp hair that curled about the temples, meant something alive and young: something that could laugh when she laughed and be merry over little things.

"Yes, of course, but not this glorious rose-pink," the young painter burst out enthusiastically. "If it will only last until I finish your portrait! It's really your month to be painted in, Mrs. Colton. You have all of Sully's harmonies in your coloring—pink, white, blue"—he was still looking into her eyes—"The great Thomas should have seen you first, I am only his humble disciple," and he shrugged his square shoulders in a modest way.

"And what about Phil?" she laughed, catching the fire of his enthusiasm as she drew the boy closer to her side.

"Well, I should try him in October. He has"—and he glanced at the Judge—"his father's brown eyes and dark skin. Nuts and autumn leaves and red berries go best with that," he added, as he ran his fingers through the boy's short curls.

"And an old fellow like me, I suppose, you'd paint with a foot of snow on the ground," laughed the Judge dryly. "Well—anything to please Olivia. Come, all of you, dinner is waiting!"

The warmth of the greeting was as great a surprise to the young Northerner as the wealth of the out-of-door bloom. He had been hospitably received in similar journeys in his own State, but never quite like this. There it was a matter of business until he had become "better acquainted," even when he stayed in the houses of his patrons. He remembered one old farmer who wanted to put him in a room over the stable with the hired man, and another, a mill-owner, who deducted the sum of his board from the price of the picture, but here he had been treated as one of the family from the moment his foot touched their door-step. The Judge had not only placed him on his right hand at table, but had sent old Bundy, the family butler, down into the wine-cellar for a bottle of old Madeira, that had "rusted away in his cellar," he said, for thirty years, and which he would open in remembrance of his college days, when his guest's uncle was his chum and classmate.

Several days had passed before he would even allow Adam to take out his brushes and prepare his canvas for work; his explanation being that as he was obliged to go on Circuit, he would like to enjoy his visitor's society before he left. There would be plenty of time for the picture while he was away. Then it too would come as a full surprise on his return—not a half-completed picture showing the work of days, but a finished portrait alive not only with the charm of the sitter, but with the genius of the master. This was proclaimed with a courteous wave of his hand to his wife and Adam, as if she, too, would be held responsible for the success of the portrait.

The morning before his departure he called Olivia

OLD-FASHIONED GENTLEMAN

and Adam, and the three made a tour of the rooms in search of a suitable place where his easel could be set up and the work begun. All three admitted that the study was too dark, and so was the library unless the vines were cleared from the windows, which was, of course, out of the question, the Judge's choice finally resting on one corner of the drawing-room, where a large window let in a little more light. In acquiescence the young painter drew back the curtains and placed his subject first on the sofa and then in an arm-chair, and again standing by the sash, and once more leaning over the window-sill; but in no position could he get what he wanted.

"Suit yourselves, then," said the Judge, "and pick out your own place, and make yourselves as comfortable as you can—only don't hurry over it. I shall not be back for a month, and if that is not time enough, why, we have all summer before us. As to your other comforts, my dear Adam—and I rejoice to see you know a good bottle of wine when you taste it—I have given Bundy express orders to decant for you some of the old Tiernan of '28, which is a little dryer than even that special bottle of the Madeira you liked so well. My only regret is that I cannot share it with you. And now one word more before I say good-by, and that is that I must ask you, my dear Gregg, to do all you can to keep Mrs. Colton from becoming lonely. You will, of course, as usual, accompany her in her afternoon rides, and I need not tell you that my own horses are at your disposal. When I return I hope to be welcomed by two Olivias; one which by your genius you will put on canvas, and the other"—and he bowed grandiloquently to his wife—"I leave in your charge."

The young painter took the first opportunity to discharge his duty—an opportunity afforded him when the Judge, after kissing his wife and shaking hands with Adam the morning he left, had stepped into his gig, his servant beside him, and with a lifting of his hat in punctilious courtesy, had driven down between the lilacs. It may have been gallantry or it may have been the pathetic way in which she waved her handkerchief in return that roused the boyish sympathy in his heart:

"Don't worry," he said in a voice full of tenderness. "He won't be long gone—only a month, he says; and don't be unhappy—I'm going to do everything to cheer you up."

"But I'm never lonely," she answered with an air of bravado, "and I try never to be unhappy. I always have Phil. And now," and she broke out into a laugh, "I have you, and that makes me feel just as I did as a girl when one of the boys came over to play with me. Come upstairs, right away, and let me show you the big garret. I'm just crazy to see you begin work, and I really believe that's the best place, after all. It's full of old trunks and furniture, but there's a splendid window——"

"On which side of the house, north or south? I must have a north light, you know."

"Yes—north; looking straight up into your freezing cold country, sir! This way! Come along!" she cried joyously as she mounted the stairs, little Phil, as usual, tumbling after them.

Adam entered first and stood in the middle of the floor looking about him.

"Superb!" he cried. "Just the very place! What a magnificent light—so direct, and not a reflection from anything."

It was, indeed, an ideal studio to one accustomed to the disorder of beautiful things. Not only was there a hip roof, with heavy, stained beams and brown shingles, but near its crotch opened a wide, round-topped window which shed its light on the dilapidated relics of two generations—old spinning-wheels, hair trunks, high-post, uncoupled bedsteads; hair-cloth sofas, and faded curtains of yellow damask, while near the door rested an enormous jar brought up from the garden to catch the drip of a leaky shingle—all so much lumber to Olivia, but of precious value to the young painter, especially the water jar, which reminded him of those he had seen in Sicily when he was tramping through its villages sketching.

"Just the place—oh, wonderful! Wonderful! Let me shout down for Bundy and we'll move everything into shape right away."

"Are you going to take them out or push them back?" exclaimed Olivia, her eyes growing wide with wonder as she watched him begin work.

"No, not going to move out one of them. You just wait—I'll show you!" The boy in him was coming out now.

And Olivia did wait, uttering little cries of delight or inquiry meanwhile, as she tripped after him, her skirts lifted above her dainty ankles to keep them from the dust. "Oh, that ugly old bureau; shan't we send it away?" followed by "Yes, I do think that's better." And, "Oh, are you going to put that screen there!" gouty old Bundy joining in with "Well, fo' de Lawd, Miss 'Livy, I neber did see no ol' truck come to life agin befo' by jes' shovin' it 'roun'."

"And now get a sheet!" cried Adam, when everything had been arranged to his liking. "We'll tack it across the lower half of the window. Then Bundy, please go down and bring up two buckets of water and pour it into this jar. Now, Mrs. Colton, come along, you and I will bring up blossoms enough to fill it," and the two dashed downstairs and out into the orchard with a swoop of two swallows out for an airing.

Even Bundy had to admit to old Dinah, when he had returned to the kitchen, that the transformation of a lumber-room into a cosy studio was little less than miraculous.

"Dat painter gemman do beat de lan'," he chuckled. "Got dat ol' garret lookin' like a parlor fixed up for comp'ny. Ye oughter see dem ol' hair-backs wid de bottoms busted—got 'em kivered up wid dem patchwork bedspreads an' lookin' like dey was fit for de ol' mist'ess's bedroom. An' he's got dem ol' yaller cut'-ains we useter hab in de settin'-room hung on de fo'-posters as sort o' screens fencin' off one corner ob de room jes' by de do'. Dat ol' carpet's spread out; dat

OLD-FASHIONED GENTLEMAN

one-legged spinnin'-wheel's propped up and standin' roun'; dem ol' stable lanterns is hung to de rafters. I clar' to goodness, ye wouldn't believe! Now dey jes' sont me down for two buckets o' water to fill dat ol' jar we useter hab settin' out here on de po'ch. He and de young mist'ess is out now lookin' for peach blossoms to fill it. He's a wonder, I tell ye!"

The masses of blossoms arranged in the big jar—the tops of their branches reaching the water-stained roof; a canvas for a half-length tacked on a stretcher and placed on an improvised easel, Adam began prying into the dark corners for a seat for his model, Olivia following his every movement, her eyes twice their usual size in her ever-increasing astonishment and delight.

"Hello, here's just the thing!" he shouted, dragging out a high-back chair with some of the lower rungs gone, and dusting it off with his handkerchief. "Sit here and let me see how the light falls. No, that isn't good; that dress won't do at all." (The gown came too far up on her neck to suit this artistic young gentleman's ideas regarding the value of curved lines in portraiture.) "That collar spoils everything. Can't you wear something else? I'd rather see you in full dress. I want the line of the throat ending in the sweep of the shoulder, and then I want the long curl against the flesh tones. You haven't worn your hair that way since I came; and where's the dress you had on the day I arrived? The colors suited you perfectly. I shall never forget how you looked—it was all blossoms, you and everything—and the background of the dark door, and the white of the porch columns, with just a touch of yellow ochre to break it— Oh, it was delicious! Please, now, put that dress on again and wear a low-neck waist with it. The flesh tones of the throat and shoulders will be superb and I know just how to harmonize them with this background."

It was the picture, not the woman, that filled his soul. Flesh tones heightened by a caressing, lingering curl, and relieved by green leaves and flowers, were what had made the Munich picture a success.

"But I haven't any low-necked gowns. Those I had when I was married are all worn out, and I've never needed any since. My nearest neighbors are ten miles away, and half the time I dine with only Phil."

"Well, but can't you fix something?" persisted Adam, bent on the composition he had in his mind. "Everybody's been so good to me here I want this portrait to be the very best I can do. What is in these trunks? There must be some old dresses belonging to somebody's grandmother or somebody's aunt. Do you mind my opening this one? It's unlocked."

Adam lifted the lid. A faded satin gown belonging to the Judge's mother lay on the top. The old lady had been born and brought up under this roof, and was still alive when the Judge's first wife died.

"Here's the very thing."

"And you really want that old frock? All right, Mr. Autocrat, I'll run down and put it on."

OLD-FASHIONED GENTLEMAN

She was like a child dressing for her first party. Twice did her hair fall about her shoulders and twice must she gather it up, fingering carefully the long curl, patting it into place; hooking the bodice so that all its modesty would be preserved and yet the line of the throat show clear, shaking out the full, pannier-like skirt until it stood out quite to her liking. Then with a mock curtsey to herself in the glass, she dashed out of the room, up the narrow stairs and into the garret again before he had had time to sort over his brushes.

"Lovely!" he burst out enthusiastically when she had whirled round so he could see all sides of her. "It's more beautiful than the one I first saw you in. Now you look like a bit of old Dresden china—No, I think you look like a little French queen. No, I don't know what you do look like, only you're the loveliest thing I ever saw!"

The gown fitted her perfectly; part of her neck was bare, the single curl, just as he wanted it, straying over it. Then came the waist of ivory-white flowered satin with elbow sleeves, and then the puffy panniers drooped about the slender bodice. As he drank in her beauty the blood went tingling through his veins. He had thought her lovely that first morning when he saw her on the porch: then she was all blossoms; now she was a vision of the olden time for whose lightest smile brave courtiers fought and bled.

"That's it, keep your head up!" he cried, as with many steppings backward and forward, he conducted her to the old chair, and with the air of a grand chamberlain placed her upon it, adding in mock gallantry:

"Sit there, fair lady mine, while your humble slave makes obeisance. To touch the hem of your garment would be— Oh, but aren't you lovely! And the tone of old ivory in the satin, and the exquisite flesh notes— and the way the curl lies on the shoulder! You are adorable!"

And so the picture was begun.

The hours and the days that followed were hours and days of never-ending joy and frolic. While it was still "Mr. Gregg" and "Mrs. Colton," it was as often "Uncle Adam" by little Phil (the three were never separated) and now and then "Marse Adam" by old Bundy, who sought in this way to emphasize his master's injunction to "look after Mr. Gregg's comfort."

Nor did the supervision stop here. Under Olivia's instructions and with Bundy's help, the big dining-room table, with the Judge's seat at one end, hers at the other, and little Phil in his high chair in the middle, was given up and moved out as being altogether too formal and the seats too far apart, and a small one, sprinkled daily with fresh damask roses that she herself had culled from the garden, was substituted. The great window in the library, which had always been kept closed by reason of a draught which carromed on the door of the study and struck the Judge somewhere between his neck and his shoulders, was now thrown wide and kept wide, and the porch chairs, three of them, which had precise positions fixed for them be-

And so the picture was begun.

tween the low windows, were dragged out under the big apple-tree shading the lawn and moved up to another table that Bundy had carried down from one of the spare rooms.

And then the joy of being for the first time the real head of the house when "company" was present—free to pour out her hospitality in her own way—free to fix the hours of breakfast, dinner, and supper, and what should be cooked, and how served; free to roam the rooms at her pleasure, in and out of the silent study without the never-infringed formality of a knock.

And the long talks in the improvised studio, she sitting under the big north window in the softened light of the sheet; the joy she took in his work; the charm of his sympathetic companionship. Then the long rides on horseback when the morning's work was over, she on Black Bess, he on his own mare; the rompings and laughter in the cool woods; the delight over the bursting of new blossoms; the budding of new leaves and tendrils, and the ceaseless song of the birds! Were there ever days like these!

And the swing and dash and freedom of it all! The perfect trust, each in the other. The absence of all coquetry and allurement, of all pretence or sham. Just chums, good fellows, born comrades; joining in the same laugh, stilled by the same thoughts; absorbed in the same incidents, no matter how trivial: the hiving of a swarm of bees, the antics of a pair of squirrels, or the unfolding of a new rose. He twenty-five, clean-souled, happy-hearted; lithe as a sapling and as graceful and full of spring. She twenty-two, soft-cheeked as a summer rose and as sweet and wholesome and as innocent of all guile as a fawn, drinking in for the first time, in unknown pastures, the fresh dew of the morning of life.

And the little comedy in the garret was played to the very end.

Each day my lady would dress herself with the greatest care in the flowered satin and coax the stray curl into position, and each day Adam would go through the ceremony of receiving her at the door with his mahlstick held before him like a staff of state. Then, bowing like a courtier, he would lead her past the yellow satin screen and big jar of blossoms and place her in the high-back chair, little Phil acting as page, carrying her train.

And so the picture was finished!

On that last day, as he stood in front of it, the light softened by the screening sheet falling full upon it, his heart swelled with pride. He knew what his brush had wrought. Not only had he given the exact pose he had labored for—the bent head, the full throat, the slope of the gently falling line from the ear to the edge of the corsage, the round of the white shoulders relieved by the caressing curl; but he had caught a certain joyous light in the eyes—a light which he had often seen in her face when, with a sudden burst of affection, she had strained little Phil to her breast and kissed him passionately.

OLD-FASHIONED GENTLEMAN

"I'm not so beautiful as that," she had said to Adam with a deprecatory tone in her voice, as the two stood before it. "It's only because you think I am, and because you've kept on saying it over and over until you believe it. It's the gown and the peach blossoms in the jar behind my chair—not me."

The servants were none the less enthusiastic. Bundy screwed up his toad eyes and expressed the opinion that it was "de 'spress image," and fat old Aunt Dinah, who had stumbled up the garret stairs from the kitchen, the first time in years—her quarters being on the ground floor of one of the cabins—put on her spectacles, and lifting up her hands, exclaimed in a camp-meeting voice:

"De Lawd wouldn't know t'other from which if both on ye went to heaben dis minute! Dat's you, sho' nuff, young mist'ess."

Only one thing troubled the young painter: What would the Judge say when he returned in the morning? What alterations would he insist upon? He had been compelled so many times to ruin a successful picture, just to please the taste of the inexperienced, that he trembled lest this, the best work of his brush, should share their fate. Should the Judge disapprove Olivia's heart would well nigh be broken, for she loved the picture as much as he did himself.

The night before Judge Colton's return the two sat out on the porch in the moonlight. The air was soft and full of the coming summer. Fire-flies darted about; the croaking of tree-toads could be heard. From the quarters of the negroes came the refrain of an old song:

> "Corn top's ripe and de meadow's in de bloom,
> Weep no mo' me lady."

"I feel as if I had been dreaming and had just waked up," sighed Olivia. "Is it all over?"

"Yes, I can't make it any better," he answered in a positive tone, his thoughts on his picture.

"Must you go away after you finish Phil's?" Her mind was not on the portrait.

"Yes, unless the Judge wants his own painted. I wish he would. I'd love to stay with you—you've been so kind to me. Nobody has ever been so good."

"And you've been very kind to me," Olivia sighed. "Oh, so kind!"

"And just think how beautiful it is here," he rejoined; "and the wonderful weather; and the lovely life we have led. You ought to be very contented in so beautiful a home, with everybody so good to you."

"It's all been very, very happy, hasn't it?" She had not listened, nor had she answered him. It was the refrain of the old song that filled her ears.

"Yes, the happiest of my life. If you'd been my own sister you couldn't have been lovelier to me."

"Where shall you go?" She was not looking at him. Her eyes were fixed on the group of trees breaking the sky line.

"Home, to my people," he answered slowly.

OLD-FASHIONED GENTLEMAN

"How far away is it?"

"Oh, a long distance! It takes me three days' constant riding to get home."

"And you love them?"

"Yes."

"Do they love you?"

"Yes."

Again the song rolled out:

> "Few mo' days to tote de weary load,
> Weep no mo' me lady."

II

The home-coming of the master brought everybody on the run to the porch: the men in the neighboring field; the gardener, who came bounding over his flower-beds; Aunt Dinah, drying her fat hands on her apron, to grasp her master's; Bundy, who helped him to alight; half a dozen pickaninnies and twice as many dogs, and last Adam and Olivia, who came flying down the front stairs, followed by little Phil.

The Judge alighted from the gig with some difficulty, Bundy guiding his foot so that it rested on the iron step, and helped him to the ground. The ride had been a trying one, and the heat and dust had left their marks on his face.

"And how about the portrait?" were his first words after kissing his wife and child and shaking hands with Gregg. "Is it finished, and are you pleased, my dear?"

"Yes, and it's lovely, only it's not me, I tell him."

"Not you? Who is it, then?"

"Oh, somebody twice as pretty!"

"No. It's not one-quarter, not one-tenth as beautiful!" There was a ring in Adam's voice that showed the tribute came from his heart.

"But that's the dress and the background; and the lovely blossoms. Oh, you'd never believe that old jar could look so well!"

AN OLD-FASHIONED GENTLEMAN

"Background! Jar! Where did you sit?" He had changed his coat now, and Bundy was brushing the dust from his trousers and shoes.

"Oh, up in the garret. You wouldn't know the place. Mr. Gregg pulled everything round until it is the cosiest room you ever saw."

The Judge shot a quick, searching glance at Adam. Then his eye took in the lithe, graceful figure of the young man, so buoyant with health and strength.

"Up in the garret! Why didn't you paint it here, or in the front room?"

"I needed a north light, sir."

"And you could only find that in a garret? I should have thought the parlor was the place for a lady. And are you satisfied with the result?" he asked in a more formal tone, as he dropped into a chair and turned to Adam. The long ride had fatigued him more than he had thought possible.

"Well, it certainly is the best thing I have ever done. The flesh tones are purer, and the——"

The Judge looked up: "Of the face?"

"All the flesh tones—especially the tones around the curl where it lies on the bare shoulder."

He was putting his best foot forward, arguing his side of the case. Half of Olivia's happiness would be gone if her husband were disappointed in the portrait.

"Let us go up and look at it," the Judge said, as if impelled by some sudden resolve.

When he reached the garret—Adam and Olivia and

little Phil had gone ahead—he stopped and looked about him.

"Well, upon my soul! You *have* turned things upside down," he remarked in a graver tone. "And here's where you two have spent all these days, is it?" Again his eye rested on Adam's graceful figure, whose cheeks were flushed with his run upstairs. With the glance came a certain feeling of revolt, as if the lad's very youth were an affront.

"Only in the morning, sir, while the light lasted," explained Adam, noticing the implied criticism in the coldness of the Judge's tones.

"Turn the picture, please, Mr. Gregg."

For a brief moment the Judge, with folded arms, gazed into the canvas; then the straight lips closed, the brow tightened, and an angry glow mounted to the very roots of his gray hair.

"Mr. Gregg," said the Judge in the same measured tone with which he would have sentenced a criminal, "if I did not know you to be a gentleman, and incapable of dishonor, I should ask you to leave my house. You may not have intended it, sir, but you have abused my hospitality and insulted my home. My wife is but a child, and easily influenced, and you should have protected her in my absence, as I would have protected yours. The whole thing is most disturbing, sir—and I——"

"Why—why—what is the matter?" gasped Adam. The suddenness of the attack had robbed him of his breath.

OLD-FASHIONED GENTLEMAN

Matter!" thundered the Judge. "Bad taste is the matter, if not worse! No woman should ever uncover her neck to any man but her husband! You have imposed upon her, sir, with your foreign notions. The picture shall never be hung!"

"But it is your own mother's dress," pleaded Olivia, a sudden flush of indignation rising in her face. "We found it in the trunk. It's on my bed now—I'll go and get it——"

"I don't want to see it! What my mother wore at her table in the presence of my father and his guests is not what she would have worn in her garret day after day for a month with her husband away. You should have remembered your blood, Olivia, and my name and position."

"Judge Colton!" cried Adam, stepping nearer and looking the Judge square in the eyes—all the forces of his soul were up in arms now—"your criticisms and your words are an insult! Your wife is as unconscious as a child of any wrong-doing, and so am I. I found the dress in the trunk and made her put it on. Mrs. Colton has been as safe here with me as if she had been my sister, and she has been my sister every hour of the day, and I love her dearly. I have told her so, and I tell you so!"

The Judge was accustomed to read the souls of men, and he saw that this one was without a stain.

"I believe you, Gregg," he said, extending his hand. "I have been hasty and have done you a wrong. Forgive me! And you, too, Olivia. I am over-sensitive about these things: perhaps, too, I am a little tired. We will say no more about it."

That night when the Judge had shut himself up in his study with his work, and Olivia had gone to her room, Adam mounted the stairs and flung himself down on one of the old sofas. The garret was dark, except where the light of the waning moon filtering through the sheet, fell upon the portrait and patterned the floor in squares of silver. Olivia's eyes still shone out from the easel. In the softened, half-ghostly light there seemed to struggle out from their depths a certain pleading look, as if she needed help and was appealing to him for sympathy. He knew it was only a trick the moonlight was playing with his colors—lowering the reds and graying the flesh tones—that when the morning came all the old joyousness would return; but it depressed him all the same.

The Judge's words with their cruelty and injustice still rankled in his heart. The quixotic protest, he knew, about his mother's faded old satin must have had some other basis than the one of immodesty—an absurd position, as any one could see who would examine the picture. Olivia could never be anything but modest. Had it really been the gown that had offended him? or had he seen something in his wife's portrait which he had missed before in her face—something of the joy which a freer and more untrammelled life had given her, and which had, therefore, aroused

OLD-FASHIONED GENTLEMAN

his jealousy. He would never forgive him for the outburst, despite the apology, nor would he ever forget Olivia cowering, when she listened, as if from a blow, hugging little Phil to her side. While the Judge's words had cut deep into his own heart they had scorched Olivia's like a flame. He had seen it in her tear-dried face seamed and crumpled like a crushed rose, when without a word to her husband or himself, except a simple—"Good-night, all," she had left the room but an hour before.

Suddenly he raised his head and listened: A step was mounting the stairs. Then came a voice from the open door.

"Adam, are you in there?"

"Yes, Olivia."

"May I come in?"

Like a wraith of mist afloat in the night she stole into the darkened room and settled slowly and noiselessly beside him. He tried to struggle to his feet in protest, but she clung to him, her fingers clutching his arm, her sobs choking her.

"Don't—don't go! I must talk to you—nobody else understands—nobody——"

"But you must not stay here! Think what——"

"No! Please—please—I can't go; you must listen! I couldn't sleep. Help me! Tell me what I must do! Oh, Adam, please—please! I shall die if I have to keep on as I have done."

She slipped from the low cushion and lay crouching at his feet, her arms and face resting on his knees; her wonderful hair, like spun gold, falling about him, its faint perfume stirring his senses.

Then, with indrawn, stifling sobs she laid bare her innermost secrets; all her heartaches, misunderstandings, hidden sorrows, and last that unnamed pain which no human touch but his could heal. Only once, as she crouched beside him, did he try to stop the flow of her whispered talk; she pleading piteously while he held her from him, he looking into her eyes as if he were afraid to read their meaning.

When she had ended he lifted her to her feet, smoothed the dishevelled hair from her face, and kissed her on the forehead:

"Go now," he said in a broken voice, as he led her to the door. "Go, and let me think it over."

With the breaking of the dawn he rose from the lounge where he had lain all night with staring eyes, took the portrait from the easel, held it for a brief instant to the gray light, touched it reverently with his lips, turned it to the wall, and then, with noiseless steps, descended to his bedroom. Gathering his few belongings together he crept downstairs so as to wake no one, pushed open the front door, crossed the porch and made his way to the stable, where he saddled his mare. Then he rode slowly past the lilacs and out of the gate.

When he reached the top of the hill and looked back, the rising sun was gilding the chimneys and

OLD-FASHIONED GENTLEMAN

quaint dormers of Derwood Manor. Only the closed shutters of Olivia's room were in shadow.

"It's the only way," he said with a sigh, and turned his horse's head towards the North.

III

The few weeks Adam Gregg spent in his father's home on his return from Derwood Manor were weeks of suffering such as he had never known in his short career. No word had come from Olivia, and none had gone from him in return. He dared not trust himself to write; he made no inquiries. He made no mention, even at home, of his visit, except to say that he had painted Judge Colton's wife and had then retraced his steps. It was not a matter to be discussed with any one—not even with his mother, to whom he told almost every happening of his life. He had seen a vision of transcendent beauty which had filled his soul. Then the curtain had fallen, blotting out the light and leaving him in darkness and despair. What was left was the memory of a tear-stained face and two pleading eyes. These would haunt him all his days.

At the end of the year he found himself in London: Gainsborough, Romney and Lawrence beckoned to him. He must master their technique, study their color. The next year was spent in Madrid studying Velasquez and Goya. It was the full brush that enthralled him now—the sweep and directness of virile methods. Then he wandered over to Granada, and so on to the coast and Barcelona, and at last to Paris.

AN OLD-FASHIONED GENTLEMAN

When his first salon picture was exhibited it could only be properly seen when the crowd opened, so great was the throng about it. It was called "A Memory," and showed the figure of a young girl standing in the sunlight with wreaths of blossoms arched above her head. On her golden hair was a wide hat which half shaded her face; one beautiful arm, exquisitely modelled and painted, rested on the neck of a black horse. A marvellous scheme of color, the critics said, the blossoms and flesh tones being wonderfully managed. No one knew the model—English, some suggested; others concluded that it was the portrait of some lady of the court in a costume of the thirties.

The day after the opening of the salon Clairin called and left his card, and the day following Fortuny mounted the stairs to shake his hand, although he had never met Gregg before. When, later on, Honorable Mention was awarded him by the jury, Boisseau, the art dealer, rang his bell and at once began to inquire about the price of portraits. Madame X. and the Countess M. had been captivated, he said, by "A "Memory," and wanted sittings. If the commissions were sufficient the dealer could arrange for very many orders, not only for many women of fashion, but of members of the Government.

The following year his portrait of Baron Chevrail received the Gold Medal and he himself a red ribbon, and a few months later his picture of "Columbus before the Council" took the highest honors at Genoa, and was bought by the Government.

During almost all the years of his triumphal progress he lived alone. So seldom was he seen outside of his studio that many of his brother painters were convinced that he never spent more than a few days at a time in Paris. They would knock, and knock again, only to be told by the concierge that monsieur was out, or in London, or on the Riviera. His studio in London and his occasional visits to Vienna, where he shared Makart's atelier while painting a portrait of one of the Austrian grand dukes, helped in this delusion. The truth was that he had no thought for things outside of his art. The rewards of fame and money never appealed to him. What enthralled him was his love of color, of harmony, of the mastering of subtleties in composition and mass. That the public approved of his efforts, and that juries awarded him honors, caused him no thrill of exultation. He knew how far short his brush had come. He was glad they liked the picture. Next time he would do better. These triumphs ruffled his surface—as a passing wind ruffles a deep pool.

As he grew in years there came a certain dignity of carriage, a certain poise of bearing. The old-time courtliness of manner was strengthened; but the sweetness of nature was still the same—a nature that won for him friends among the best about him. Not many —only three or four who had the privilege of knocking with three light taps and one loud one at his door, a signal to which he always responded—but friends whose proudest boast was their intimacy with Adam Gregg.

OLD-FASHIONED GENTLEMAN

The women smiled at him behind their lorgnons as they passed him riding in the Bois, for he had never given up this form of out-door exercise, his erect military figure, fine head and upturned mustache lending him a distinction which attracted attention at once; but he seldom did more than return their salutations. Sometimes he would accept an invitation to dinner, but only on rare occasions. When he did it was invariably heralded in advance that "Gregg was coming," a fact which always decided uncertain guests to say "Yes" to their hostess's invitation.

And yet he was not a recluse in the accepted sense of the word, nor did he lead a sad life. He only preferred to enjoy it alone, or with one or two men who understood him.

While casual acquaintances—especially those in carriages—were denied access when he was absorbed on some work of importance, the younger painters—those who were struggling up the ladder—were always welcome. For these the concierge was given special instructions. Then everything would be laid aside; their sketches gone over and their points settled, no matter how long it took or how many hours of his precious time were given to their service. Many of these lads—not alone his own countrymen, but many who could not speak his language—often found a crisp, clean bank-note in their hands when the painter's fingers pressed their own in parting. Of only one thing was he intolerant, and that was sham. The insincere, the presuming and the fraudulent always irritated him;

so did the slightest betrayal of a trust. Then his dark-brown eyes would flash, his shoulders straighten, and there would roll from his lips a denunciation which those who heard never forgot—an outburst all the more startling because coming from one of so gentle and equable a temperament.

During all the years of his exile no word had come from Olivia. He had once seen Judge Colton's name in one of the Paris papers in connection with a railroad case in which some French investors were interested, but nothing more had met his eye.

Had he been of a different temperament he would have forgotten her and that night in the improvised studio, but he was not constituted to forget. He was constituted to remember, and to remember with all his soul. Every day of his life he had missed her; never was there a night that she was not in his thoughts before he dropped to sleep. What would have been his career had fate brought them together before the blight fell upon her? What intimacies, what enjoyment, what ideals nurtured and made real. And the companionship, the instant sympathy, the sureness of an echo in her heart, no matter how low and soft his whisper! These thoughts were never absent from his mind.

Moreover, his life had been one of standards: the greatest painter, the greatest picture, the finest piece of bronze. It was so when he looked over curios at the dealer's: it was the choicest of its kind that he must have; anything of trifling value, or anything common-

OLD-FASHIONED GENTLEMAN

place—he ignored. Olivia had also fixed for him a standard. Compared to her, all other women were trite and incomplete. No matter how beautiful they might be, a certain simplicity of manner was lacking, or the coloring was bad, or the curve of the neck ungraceful. All of these perfections, and countless more, made up Olivia's personality, and unless the woman before him possessed these several charms she failed to interest him. The inspection over and the mental comparison at an end, a straightening of the shoulders and a knitting of the brow would follow, ending in a far-away look in his brown eyes and an unchecked sigh —as if the very hopelessness of the comparison brought with it a certain pain. As to much of the life of the Quartier about him, he shrank from it as he would from a pestilence. Certain men never crossed his threshold —never dared.

One morning there came to him the crowning honor of his career. A new hôtel de ville was about to be erected in a neighboring city, and the authorities had selected him to paint the great panel at the right of the main entrance. As he threw the letter containing the proposition on his desk and leaned back in his chair a smile of supreme satisfaction lighted up his face. He could now carry out a scheme of color and massing of figures which had been in his mind for years, but which had heretofore been impossible owing to the limited area covered by the canvases of his former orders. This space would give him all the room he needed. The subject was to be an incident in the life of Ro-

THE ROMANCE OF AN

chambeau, just before the siege of Yorktown. Gregg had been selected on account of his nationality. Every latitude was given him, and the treatment was to be distinctly his own.

It was while searching about the streets and cafés of Paris for types to be used in the preliminary sketches for this, the supreme work so far of his life, that he took a seat one afternoon in the early autumn at a table outside one of the cheap cafés along the Seine. He could study the faces of those passing, from a position of this kind. In his coming picture there must necessarily be depicted a group of the great Frenchman's followers, and a certain differentiation of feature would be necessary. On this afternoon, then, he had taken his sketch-book from his breast pocket and was about to make a memorandum of some type that had just attracted him, when a young man in a student's cap twisted his head to get a closer view of the work of Gregg's pencil.

An intrusion of this kind from any one but a student would have been instantly resented by Adam. Not so, however, with the young fellow at his elbow; these were his wards, no matter where he met them.

"Come closer, my boy," said Gregg in a low voice. "You belong to the Quartier, do you not?"

"Yes."

"Are you English?"

"No, an American. I am from Maryland."

"From Maryland, you say!" exclaimed Adam with a sudden start, closing his sketch-book and slipping it

OLD-FASHIONED GENTLEMAN

into his pocket. The name always brought with it a certain rush of blood to his cheek—why, he could never tell. "How long have you been in Paris, my lad?" He had moved back now so that the stranger could find a seat beside him.

"Only a few months, sir. I was in London for a time and then came over here. I'm working at Julian's"—and the young fellow squeezed himself into the chair Adam had pulled out for him.

"Are you from one of the cities?"

"No, from Montgomery County, sir."

"That's next to Frederick, isn't it?"

"Yes, sir."

Both question and answer set his pulses to beating. Instantly there rushed into his mind the picture he never forgot—the figure in white standing at the head of the porch steps. He recalled the long curl that lay next her throat, the light in her eyes, the warm pressure of her hand; the wealth of bursting blossoms, their perfume filling the spring air. How many years had passed since he had ridden through those Maryland orchards!

For some minutes Adam sat perfectly still, his eyes fixed on the line of trees fringing the parapet of the Seine. The boy kept silent; it was for the older man to speak first again. Soon an overwhelming, irresistible desire to break through the reserve of years surged over the painter. He could ask this lad questions he had never asked any one before—not that he had ever had an opportunity, for he had seen no one who knew, and he had determined never to write. Here was his chance.

"Perhaps you can tell me about some of the old residents. I visited your part of the State many years ago—in the spring, I remember—and met a few of the people. What has become of Major Dorsey, Mr. Talbot and"—there was a slight pause—"and Judge Colton?"

"I don't know, sir. I've heard my father speak of them, but I never saw any of them except Judge Colton. He used to stay at our house when he held court. He lived up in Frederick County—a thin, solemn-looking man, with white hair. He's dead now."

Gregg's fingers tightened convulsively. "Judge Colton dead! Are you sure?"

"Yes—died the week I left home. Father went up to his funeral. He rode in the carriage with Mrs. Colton, he told us when he came home. They're pretty poor up there, too; the Judge lost all his money, I heard."

Gregg paid for his coffee, rose from his seat, shook hands with the boy, gave him his name and address in case he ever wanted advice or help and continued his walk under the trees overlooking the river. The news had come to him out of the sky, and in a way that partook almost of the supernatural. There was no doubt in his mind of the truth. The boy's Southern accent and his description of the man who ten years before had denounced Olivia and himself, was confirmation enough.

OLD-FASHIONED GENTLEMAN

As he forged along, elbowing his way among the throng that crowded the sidewalk, the scene in the garret the night he parted from Olivia took possession of him—the one scene in all their past relation on which he never allowed himself to dwell. He recalled the tones of her voice, the outline of her figure crouching at his knees, the squares of moonlight illumining the floor and the room, and now once again he listened to the story she had poured into his ears that fatal night.

By the time he had reached his studio his mind was made up. Olivia was in trouble, perhaps in want. In the conditions about her she must be threatened by many dangers and must suffer many privations. The old ungovernable longing again gripped him, and with renewed force.

What was there in life but love? he said to himself. What else counted? What were his triumphs, his honors, his position among his brother painters, his welcome among his equals, compared to the love of this woman? What happiness had they brought him? Then his mind reverted to his past life. How hungry had he been for the touch of a hand, the caress of a cheek, the whispered talk into responsive ears. No! there was nothing—nothing but love! Everything else was but the ashes of a bitter fruit.

He must see Olivia, and at once; the long wait was over now. What her attitude of mind might be made no difference, or what her feeling towards him for deserting her on that terrible night. To-day she was

AN OLD-FASHIONED GENTLEMAN

unprotected, perhaps in want. To help her was a matter of honor.

With these thoughts crowding out every other, and with the impetus of the resolve hot upon him, he opened his portfolio and wrote a note, informing the committee in charge of the Rochambeau picture of his sudden departure for America and the consequent impossibility of executing the commission with which they had honored him.

Three days later, with a new joy surging through his veins, he set sail for home.

IV

Again Adam drew rein and looked over the brown hills of Maryland. No wealth of bursting blossoms greeted him; the trees were bare of leaves, their naked branches shivering in the keen November wind; in the dips of the uneven roads the water lay in pools; above hung a dull, gray sky telling of the coming cold; long lines of crows were flying southward, while here and there a deserted cabin showed the havoc the years of war had wrought—a havoc which had spared neither friend nor foe.

None of these things disturbed Adam nor checked the flow of his spirits. The cold would not reach his heart; there was a welcome ahead—of eye and hand and heart. No word of him had reached her ears. If she had forgiven him, thought of him at all, it was as across the sea in some unknown land. Doubtless she still believed he had forgotten her and their early days. This would make the surprise he held in store for her all the more joyous.

As he neared the brow of the hill he began to con over in his mind the exact words he would use when he was ushered into her presence. He would pretend at first to be a wayfarer and ask for a night's lodging, or, perhaps, it might be best to inquire for young Phil, who must now be a great strapping lad. Then he began thinking out other surprises. Of course she would know him—know him before he opened his lips. How foolish, then, the pretence of deceiving her. What was really more important was the way in which he would enter the house; some care must therefore be exercised. If he should approach by the rear and meet either Dinah or old Bundy, who must still be alive, of course they would recognize him at once before he could caution them, the back door being near the old kitchen. The best way would be to signal Bundy and call to him before the old man could fully identify him. He could then open the door softly and step in front of her.

Perhaps another good way would be to leave his horse in the stable, and wait until it grew quite dark—the twilight was already gathering—watch the lights being lit, and in this way discover in which room she was sitting. Then he would creep under the window and sing the old song they had listened to so often together, "Weep no mo', me lady." She would know then who had come all these miles to see her!

Soon his mind ran riot over the gown she would wear; how her hair would be dressed—would she still be the same slight, graceful woman, or had the years left their mark upon her? The eyes would be the same, he knew, and the lips and dazzling teeth; and she would greet him with that old fearless look in her face—courage and gentleness combined—but would there be any lines about the dear mouth and under the

OLD-FASHIONED GENTLEMAN

eyes? If so would she be willing to let him smooth them out? She was free now! Both were—free to come and go without restraint. What would he not do for her! All her future and his own would hereafter be linked together. His life, his triumphs, his honors—everything would be hers!

As these thoughts filled his mind something of the spring and buoyancy of his earlier youth came back to him. He could hardly restrain himself from shouting out in glee as he had done in the old days when they had scampered through the woods together. With each familiar spot his enthusiasm increased. There was the brook where they fished that morning for gudgeons, when little Phil came so near falling into the water; and there was the turn of the road that led to the school-house; and the little cabin near the spring. It would not be long now before he looked into her eyes!

The few friends who knew him as a grave and thoughtful man of purpose and achievement would never have recognized him could they have watched his face as he sat astride his horse, his whole body quivering with expectancy, the hope that had lain dormant so long awake once more. Now it was his turn to be glad.

He had reached the hill. Another moment and he would pass the mass of evergreens to the left, and then the quaint dormer-windows and chimneys of Derwood Manor would greet him.

At the bend of the road, on the very verge of the hill,

he checked his horse so suddenly as almost to throw him back on his haunches. A sudden chill seized him, followed by a rush that sent the blood tingling to the roots of his hair. Then he stood up in his stirrups as if to see the better.

Below, against the background of ragged trees, stood two gaunt chimneys. All about was blackened grass and half-burned timbers.

Derwood Manor had been burned to the ground!

Staggered by the sight, almost reeling from the saddle, he drove the spurs into his horse, dashed through the ruined gate, and drew rein at the one unburned cabin. A young negro woman stood in the door.

For an instant he could hardly trust himself to speak.

"I am Mr. Gregg," he said in a choking voice, "and was here ten years ago. When did this happen?" and he pointed to the blackened ruins. He had thrown himself from his saddle and stood looking into her face, the bridle in his hand.

"In de summer time—las' August, I think."

"Where's your mistress? Was she here when the house was burned?"

"I ain't got no mist'ess—not now. Oh, you mean de young mist'ess what used to lib here? Aunt Dinah cooked for 'em—she b'longed to 'em."

"Yes, yes," urged Gregg.

"She's daid!"

"My God! Not when the house was burned?"

"No, she warn't here. She was down in Baltimo' —she went dar after de Jedge died. But she's daid,

OLD-FASHIONED GENTLEMAN

fo' sho', 'cause Aunt Dinah was wid her, and she tol' me."

Adam dropped upon a bench outside the door of the cabin and began passing his hand nervously over his forehead as if he would relieve a pain he could not locate. A cold sweat stood on his brow; his knees shook.

The woman kept her eyes on him. Such incidents were not uncommon. Almost every day strangers on their way South had passed her cabin, looking for friends they would never see again—a woman for her husband; a mother for her son; a father for his children. Unknown graves and burned homes could be found all the way to the Potomac and beyond. This strong man who seemed to be an officer, was like all the others.

For some minutes Adam sat with his head in his hand; his elbows on his knees, the bridle still hooked over his wrist. Hot tears trickled between his closed fingers and dropped into the dust at his feet. Then he raised his head, and with a strong effort pulled himself together.

"And the little boy—or rather the son—he must be grown now. Philip was his name—what has become of him?" He had regained something of his old poise—his voice and manner showed it.

"I ain't never yeard what 'come 'o him. Went in de army, I reck'n. Daid, I spec'—mos' ev'ybody's daid dat was here when I growed up."

Adam turned his head and looked once more at the

AN OLD-FASHIONED GENTLEMAN

blackened ruins. What further story was yet to come from their ashes?

"One more question, please. Were you here when the fire came?"

"Yes, suh, me and my husban' was both here. He ain't home to-day. We was takin' care of de place when it ketched fire—dat's how we come to save dis cabin. Dere warn't no water and nobody to help, and dis was all we could do."

Again Adam bowed his head. Was there nothing left?—nothing to recall even her smile? Then slowly, as if he feared the result:

"Was anything saved—any furniture, or—pictures —or——"

"Nothin' but dem two chairs inside dar—and dat bench what you's settin' on. Dey was on de lawn and dat's how we come to git 'em."

For some minutes Adam sat looking into the ground at his feet, his eyes blurred with tears.

"Thank you," was all he said.

And once more he turned his horse's head towards the North.

V

A thin, shabby little man, with stooping shoulders, hooked nose and velvet tread, stood before the card rack in the lower corridor of the old studio building on Tenth Street. He was scanning the names, beginning at the top floor and going down to the basement. Suddenly his eyes glistened:

"Second floor," he whispered to himself. "Yes, of course; I knew it all the time—second floor," and "second floor" he kept repeating as he helped his small body up the steps by means of the hand-rail.

The little man earned his living by obtaining orders for portraits which he turned over to the several painters, fitting the price to their reputations, and by hunting up undoubted old masters, rare porcelains, curios and miniatures for collectors. He was reasonably honest, and his patrons followed his advice whenever it was backed by somebody they knew. He was also cunning—softly, persuasively cunning—with all the patience and philosophy of his race.

On this morning the little man had a Gilbert Stuart for sale, and what was more to the point he had a customer for the masterpiece: Morlon, the collector, of unlimited means and limited wall space, would buy it provided Adam Gregg, the distinguished portrait painter, Member of the International Jury, Commander of the Legion of Honor, Hors Concours in Paris and Munich, etc., etc., would pronounce it genuine.

The distinguished painter never hesitated to give his services in settling such matters. He delighted in doing it. Just as he always delighted in criticising the work of any young student who came to him for counsel—a habit he had learned in his life abroad—and always with a hand on the boy's shoulder and a twinkle in his brown eyes that robbed his words of any sting.

When dealers sought his help he was not so gracious. He disliked dealers—another of his foreign prejudices. Tender-hearted as he was he generally exploded with dynamic force—and he could explode when anything stirred him—whenever a dealer attempted to make him a party to anything that looked like fraud. He had once cut an assumed Corot into ribbons with his pocket-knife—and this since he had been home in New York, fifteen years now—and had then handed the strips back to the dealer with the remark:

"Down in the Treasury they brand counterfeits with a die; I do it with a knife. Send me the bill."

The little man, with the cunning of his race, knew this peculiarity, and he also knew that ten chances to one the great painter would receive him with a frigid look, and perhaps bow him out of the door. So he had studied out and arranged a little game. Only the day before he had obtained an order for a portrait to be painted by the best man-painter of his time. The

OLD-FASHIONED GENTLEMAN

picture was to be full length and to hang in the directors' room of a great corporation. This order he had in his pocket in writing, signed by the secretary of the board. Confirmations were sometimes valuable.

As the little man's body neared the great painter's door a certain pleasurable sensation trickled through him. To catch a painter on a hook baited with an order, and then catch a great collector like Morlon on another hook baited with a painter, was admirable fishing.

With these thoughts in his mind he rapped timidly on Adam Gregg's door, and was answered by a strong, cheery voice calling:

"Come in!"

The door swung back, the velvet curtains parted, and the little man made a step into the great painter's spacious studio.

"Oh, I have such a fine sitter for you!" he whispered, with his hand still grasping the curtain. "Such a distinguished-looking man he is—like a pope—like a doge. It will make a great Franz Hal; such a big spot of white hair and black coat and red face. He's coming to-morrow and——"

"Who is coming to-morrow?" asked Gregg. His tone would have swamped any other man. He had recognized the dealer with a simple "Good-morning," and had kept his place before his easel, the overhead light falling on his upturned mustache and crisp gray hair.

The little man rubbed his soft, flabby hands together, and tiptoed to where Gregg stood as noiseless as a detective approaching a burglar.

"The big banker," he whispered. "Did you not get my letter? The price is no object. I can show you the order." He had reached the easel now and was standing with bent head, an unctuous smile playing about his lips.

"No, I don't want to see it," remarked Gregg, squeezing a tube on his palette. "I can't reach it for some time, you know."

"Yes, I have told them so, but the young gentleman wants to have the entry made on the minutes and have the money appropriated. I had great confidence, you see, in your goodness," and the little man touched his forehead with one skinny finger and bowed obsequiously.

"I thought you said he had white hair."

"So he has. The portrait is to hang up in the directors' room of one of the big copper companies. The young gentleman is a member of the banking firm that is to pay for the picture, and is quite a young man. He buys little curios of me now and then, and he asked me whom I would recommend to paint the director's portrait, and, of course, there is but one painter—" and the dealer bowed to the floor. "He's coming to-morrow afternoon at four o'clock and will stay but a moment, for he's a very busy man. You will, I know, receive him."

Gregg made no reply. Rich directors did not appeal to him; they were generally flabby and well fed

OLD-FASHIONED GENTLEMAN

and out of drawing. If this one had some color in him —and the dealer knew—some of the sort of vigor and snap that would have appealed to Franz Hal, the case might be different. The little man waited a moment, saw that Gregg was absorbed in some brush stroke, and stepped back a pace or two. Better wait until the master's mind was free. Then again he could sweep his eyes around the interior without being detected— there was no telling what might happen: some day there might be a sale, and then it would be just as well to know where things like these could be found. Again he tiptoed across the spacious room, stopping to gaze at the rich tapestries lining the walls, examining with eye-glass held close the gold snuffboxes and rare bits of Sèvres and Dresden on the shelves of the cabinet, and testing with his nervous fingers the quality of the rich Utrecht velvet screening the door of an adjoining room.

Gregg kept at work, his square, strong shoulders, well-knit back and straight limbs—a fulfilment of the promise of his youth—in silhouette against the glare of the overhead light, its rays silvering his iron-gray hair and the tips of his upturned mustache.

The tour of the room complete, the little man again bowed to the floor and said in his softest voice:

"And you will receive him at four o'clock?"

"Yes, at four o'clock," answered Gregg, his eyes still on the canvas.

Again the little man's head bent low as he backed from the room. There was no need of further talk.

What Adam Gregg meant he said, and what he said he meant. As he reached the velvet curtain through which he had entered, he stopped.

"And now will you do something for me?"

Gregg lifted his chin with the movement of a big mastiff throwing up his head when he scents danger. "I was waiting for that; then there is a string to it?" he laughed.

The little man reddened to his eyebrows. The fish had not only seen the hook under the bait, but knew who held the line.

"No, only that you come with me to Schenck's to see a portrait by Gilbert Stuart," he pleaded. "I quite forgot—it is not often I do forget; I must be getting old. It's to be sold to-morrow; Mr. Morlon will buy it if you approve; he said so. I'm just from his house."

"I have a sitter at three."

"Yes, I know, but you always have a sitter. You must come—it means something to me. I'll go and get a cab. It will not take half an hour. It is such a beautiful Stuart. There's no doubt about it, not the slightest; only you know Mr. Morlon, he's very exacting. He says, 'If Mr. Gregg approves I will buy it.' These were his very words."

Gregg laid down his brushes. Little men like the one before him wasted his time and irritated him. It was always this way—some underhand business. Then the better side of him triumphed.

"All right!" he cried, the old sympathetic tone ringing out once more in his voice. "Never mind about the cab; I need the air and the walk will do me good; and then you know I can't see Mr. Morlon swindled," and he laughed merrily as he looked quizzically at the dealer.

The entrance of the distinguished painter into the gallery of the auctioneer with his quick, alert manner and erect, military bearing, the Legion of Honor in his lapel, soon attracted attention. Schenck came up and shook Gregg's hands cordially, repeating his name aloud so that every one could hear it—especially the prospective buyers, some of whom gazed after him, remarking to their fellows, as they shielded their lips with their catalogues: "That's Gregg!"—a name which needed no further explanation.

"I have come to look at a Stuart that Mr. Morlon wants to buy if it is genuine," said Gregg. "Tell me what you know about it. Where did it come from?"

"I don't know; it was left on storage and is to be sold for expenses."

"Is it to be sold to the highest bidder?"

"No, at private sale."

"Where is it?"

"There—behind you."

Gregg turned and caught his breath.

Before him was a portrait of a young woman in an old-fashioned gown, her golden hair enshrining a face of marvellous beauty, one long curl straying down a shoulder of exquisite mould and finish, the whole relieved by a background of blossoms held together in a quaint earthen jar.

Strong man as he was, the shock almost overcame him. He reached out his hand and grasped the back of a chair. Tears welled up in his eyes.

The auctioneer had been watching him closely.

"You seem to like it, Mr. Gregg."

"Yes," answered Adam in restrained, measured tones. "Yes, very much. But you have been misinformed; it is not by Gilbert Stuart. It is by a man I know, I saw him paint it. Tell Mr. Morlon so. Send it to my studio, please, and credit this gentleman with the commission—I'll buy it for old association's sake."

That night, when it grew quite dark, he took the portrait from where the cartman had left it in his studio with its face to the wall—never again would it suffer that indignity—and placed it under his skylight. He wanted to see what the fading light would do—whether the changed colors would once more unlock the secrets of a soul. Again, as in the dim shimmer of the dawn, there struggled out from the wonderful eyes that same pleading look—the look he had seen on its face the morning he had left Derwood Manor—as if she needed help and was appealing to him for sympathy. Then he flashed up the circle of gas jets, flooding the studio with light. Instantly all her joyousness returned. Once more there shone out the old happy smile and laughing eyes. Loosening the nails that held the canvas, he freed the portrait from its gaudy frame, and

OLD-FASHIONED GENTLEMAN

with the remark—"It was unframed when I kissed it last," placed it over the mantel moving some curios out of the way so it would rest the more firmly; then he dropped into a chair before it.

He was in the past again—twenty-five years before, living once more the long hours in the garret with its background of blossoms; roaming the woods; listening to the sound of her joyous laughter when she caught little Phil to her breast Then there rang in his ear that terrible moan when Judge Colton denounced them both; and the sob in her voice as she sank at his feet that night. He could catch the very perfume of her hair and feel the hot tears on his hand. If only the lips would open and once more whisper his name! What had sent her back, to soothe him with her beauty?

His whole life passed in review—his hopes, his ambitions, his struggles; the years of loneliness, of misunderstanding, and the final triumph—a triumph made all the more bitter by a fate which had prevented her sharing it with him. With this there arose in his mind the picture of two gaunt chimneys outlined against a cold, gray sky; the trees bare of leaves, the grass shrivelled and brown—and then, like a refrain, came the long-forgotten song:

"Weep no mo', me lady."

Raising himself to his feet he leaned over the mantel and looked long and steadily into the eyes of the portrait.

"Olivia," he whispered—in a voice that was barely

AN OLD-FASHIONED GENTLEMAN

audible—"I did not intend to be cruel. Forgive me, dear; there was nothing else to do—it was the only way, my darling!"

He was still in his chair, the studio a blaze of light, when a brother painter from the studio opposite, whose knock had been unheeded, pushed open the door. Even then Gregg did not stir until the intruder laid a hand upon his shoulder.

VI

By noon the next day half the occupants of the old studio building came in to see the new portrait. He had not told of this one, but the brother painter had spread the news of the "find" through the building.

It was not the first time Adam Gregg's "finds" had been the subject of discussion among his fellows. The sketch by Velasquez—now the pride of the gallery that owned it—and which had been discovered by him in a lumber-room over a market, and the Romney which had been doing duty as a chimney-screen, had been the talk of the town for weeks.

"Looks more like a Sully than a Stuart," said the brother painter, his eyes half closed to get the better effect. "Got all Sully's coloring."

"Stunning girl, anyway; doesn't make any difference who painted it," suggested another. "That kind seem to have died out. You read about them in books, but I've never met one."

"Wonderful flesh," remarked a third with meaning in his voice. "If it isn't by Sully it's by somebody who believed in him."

No one suspected Gregg's brush. His style had changed with the years—so had his color: that palette had been set with the yellow, red, and blue of sunshine, blossom and sky, and the paints had been mixed with laughter. Nor did he tell them he himself had painted it. This part of his life was guarded with the same care with which he would have guarded his mother's secrets. Had he owned a shrine he would have placed the picture over its altar that he might kneel before it.

"These blue-eyed blondes," continued the first speaker meditatively with his eyes on the portrait, "send a lot of men to the devil."

Gregg looked up, but made no reply. Both the tone of the man and his words jarred on him.

"You can forget a brunette," he went on, "no matter how bewitching she may be, but one of these peaches-and-cream girls—the blue-eyed, red-lipped, white-skinned combination—takes hold of a fellow. This man knew all about it—" and he waved his hand at the portrait.

"Is that all you see in it?" rejoined Gregg coldly. "Is there nothing under the paint that appeals to you? Something of the soul of the woman?"

"Yes, and that's just what counts in these blondes; that 'soul' you talk about. That's what makes 'em dangerous. That's what captured Hartman, I guess. Mrs. Bowdoin's got just that girl's coloring—not so pretty," and he glanced at the canvas, "but along her lines. Old man Bowdoin says he's ruined his home."

"Yes, and it's pretty rough I tell you on the old man," remarked a third. "I saw him yesterday. The poor fellow is all broken up. There's going to be

OLD-FASHIONED GENTLEMAN

a row, and a hot one, I hear. Pistols, divorce; the air's blue; all sorts of things. Old fellow blusters, but he looks ten years older."

Gregg had risen from his chair and stood facing the speaker, his brown eyes flashing, his lips quivering. The talk had drifted in a direction that set his blood to tingling.

"You tell me that Hartman has at last run away with Mrs. Bowdoin!" he exclaimed angrily, his voice rising in intensity as he proceeded. "Has he finally turned scoundrel and made an outcast of himself and of her? I have been expecting something of the kind ever since I saw him in Bowdoin's studio at his last reception. And do you really mean to tell me that he has actually run off with her?"

"Well, not exactly run off—she's gone to her mother. She's only half Bowdoin's age, you know. Hartman, of course, pooh-poohs the whole thing."

"And he's Bowdoin's friend, I suppose you know!" Gregg continued in a restrained, incisive tone.

"Yes, certainly, studied with him; that's where he met her so often."

Gregg began pacing the floor. Stopping short in his walk he turned and faced the group about the fire:

"Does he realize," he burst out in a voice that rang through the room and fastened every eye upon him— "what his cowardly weakness will bring him? The misery it will entail; the sleepless nights, the fear, the remorse that will follow? The outrage on Bowdoin's home, on his children? Has he thought of the humiliation of the man deserted—the degradation of the man who caused it? Does he know what it is to live a life where every decent woman brands you as a scoundrel, and every decent man looks upon you as a thief?"

The outburst astounded the room. One or two arose from their chairs and stood looking at him in amazement. Gregg was often outspoken; right was right with him, and wrong was wrong, and he never minced matters. They loved him for his frankness and courage, but this outbreak seemed entirely uncalled for by anything that had been said or done. Surely there must be a personal side to his attitude. Had any friend of his any such experience that he should explode so suddenly? What made it all the more unaccountable was that he never talked gossip, and never allowed any man to speak ill of a friend in his presence, no matter what the cause—and Hartman was his friend. Why, then, should he pounce upon him without proof of any kind other than the gossip of the studios?

"Well, my dear Gregg, don't blame me," laughed the painter who had borne the brunt of the outbreak and whom Adam had singled out to listen to his attack. "I haven't run off with pretty Mrs. Bowdoin, or made love to her either, have I?"

"But you still shake hands with Hartman, don't you?"

"Of course I do. I couldn't show him the door, could I? He's made an ass of himself, but it's none of my business. They'll have to patch it up between

OLD-FASHIONED GENTLEMAN

them. Don't get excited, Gregg, and don't forget that the jury meets this afternoon at four o'clock in my studio."

"I will be there," replied Adam curtly, "but I cannot stay very long. I have an appointment at four."

The room was full of his brother painters when, some hours later, his red Spanish *boina* on his head—he always wore it when at work—Gregg entered the studio on the floor below his own. It was the first informal meeting of the Jury of the Academy, and an important one. Some of the men were grouped about the fire, smoking, or lolling in their chairs; others were stretched out on the lounges; two or three were looking over some etchings that had been brought in by a fellow-member. All had been awaiting Adam's arrival. Those who had been gathered about the portrait were discussing Gregg's denunciation of Hartman. All agreed that with their knowledge of the man's universal kindness and courtesy that the outburst was as unaccountable as it was astounding.

Gregg shook hands with the group, one by one, those who were reclining rising to their feet and the others pressing forward to greet him; then drawing out a chair at the end of the long table, he called the meeting to order. As he took his seat a man of thirty in an overcoat, his hat in his hand, walked hurriedly in through the open door, and stood for a moment looking about him, a sickly, wavering expression on his face, as if uncertain of his welcome. It was Hartman.

He was a member of the Council, and therefore privileged to attend any meeting.

Gregg pushed back his chair and rose to his feet, a certain flash of indignation in his eyes that few of his friends had ever seen.

"Stop where you are, Mr. Hartman," he said in low, cutting tones. "I prefer to conduct this meeting without you."

"And I prefer to stay where I am," answered Hartman in an unsteady voice, gazing about as if in search of some friendly eye. "I have as much right to be at this meeting as you have," he continued, advancing towards the pile of coats and hats.

Adam was in front of him now, his big, broad frame almost touching the intruder. The quick, determined movement meant danger. No one had ever seen Gregg so stirred.

"You will do as I tell you, sir! Leave the room—now—at once! Do you hear me!"

Every man was on his feet. Those who had heard Gregg's outburst a few hours before knew the reason. Others were entirely ignorant of the cause of his wrath.

"You are not responsible for me or my actions. I'm a man who can——"

"Man! You are not a man, sir! You are a thief, one who steals into a brother painter's home and robs him of everything he holds dear. Get out of here! Go and hide yourself in the uttermost parts of the earth where no man you ever saw will know you!

OLD-FASHIONED GENTLEMAN

Jump into the sea—destroy yourself! Go, you leper! Savages protect their women!"

He had his fingers in Hartman's collar now and was backing him towards the door. One or two men tried to stop him, but Gregg's voice rang out clear:

"Keep your hands off! Out he goes, if I have to throw him downstairs. Stand back, all of you—" and with a mighty effort he caught the younger and apparently stronger man under the armpits and hurled him through the open doorway.

For some seconds no one spoke. The suddenness of the attack, the uncontrollable anger of the distinguished painter—so gentle and forbearing always—the tremendous strength of the man; the cowering look on Hartman's face—a look that plainly told of his guilt—had stunned every one in the room.

Gregg broke the silence. He had locked the door on Hartman and was again in his chair by the table, a flushed face and rumpled shirt the only marks of the encounter.

"I owe you an apology, gentlemen," he said, adjusting his cuffs and speaking in the same voice with which he would have asked for a match to light his cigar. "I did not intend to disturb the meeting, but there are some things I cannot stand. We have curs prowling around in society, walking in and out of decent homes, trusted and believed in, that are twice as dangerous as mad dogs. Hartman is one of them. When they bite they kill. The only way is to shut your doors in their faces. That I shall do whenever one crosses my path. And now, if you will excuse me, I will ask one of you to fill my place and let me go back to my studio. I have an appointment at four, as I told you this morning, and I'm late."

Once in the corridor he stepped to the rail, looked over the banisters as if in expectation of seeing the object of his wrath, and slowly mounted the stairs to his studio. As he approached the velvet curtain he heard through the half-closed door a heavy step. Some one was walking about inside. Was Hartman waiting for him to renew the conflict? he wondered. Pushing aside the curtain he stepped boldly in.

On the mat before the fire, with his back to the door, his eyes fixed on Olivia's portrait, stood a young man he had never seen before. As the overhead light fell on his glossy hair and over his clean-shaven face and well-groomed body, Gregg noticed that he belonged to the class of prosperous business men of the day. This was not only apparent in the way his well-cut clothes fitted his slender body—perfect in appointment, from the bunch of violets in his button-hole to his polished shoes—but in his quick movements.

"Have I made a mistake?" the young man asked in a crisp, decisive voice. "This is Mr. Adam Gregg, is it not? I found your door on a crack and thought you were not far off."

"No, you haven't made a mistake," answered Adam courteously, startled out of his mood by the bearing and kindly greeting of the stranger. "My

OLD-FASHIONED GENTLEMAN

name is Gregg—what can I do for you?" All trace of his former agitation was gone now.

"Well, I am here on behalf of my special partner, Mr. Eggleston, who is also a director in one of our companies, and who had an appointment with you at four o'clock. He is detained at the trust company's office, and I came in his stead. The portrait, as I suppose that little fellow—I forget his name—has told you, is to hang up in the office of the Portage Copper Company—that's our company. We want a full-sized portrait—big and important. Mr. Eggleston is a good deal of a man, you know, and there's a business side to it—business side to most everything in the Street," this came with a half-laugh. "I'll tell you about that later. You never saw him, of course. No?—he's so busy he doesn't get around much uptown. Fine, large, rather imposing-looking—white hair, red face and big hands—lots of color about him—ought to paint him, I suppose, with his hand on a globe, or some books. I'm not posted on these things, but you'll know when you see him. He'll be up any day next week that you say. We want it right away, of course. Some business in that, too," and another faint laugh escaped his lips.

All this time Gregg had been standing in front of the stranger waiting for an opportunity to offer him his hand and tell how sorry he was to have kept him waiting, explaining the meeting of the jury and his being obliged to be present, but the flow of talk had continued without a break and in a way that began to attract his attention.

THE ROMANCE OF AN

"Got a nice place here," the young man rattled on, gazing about him as he spoke; "first time I was ever in a studio, and first time, too, I ever met a real painter in his workshop. I'm so tied down. Valuable, these things you've got here, too—cost a lot of money. I buy a few myself now and then. By the bye, while I was waiting for you to come in I couldn't help looking at the pictures and things."

He had stepped closer now, his eyes boring into Gregg's as if he were trying to read his mind. For an instant Gregg thought an extra cocktail on the way uptown was the cause of his garrulousness.

"Of course I know it's all right, Mr. Gregg, or you wouldn't have it—and you needn't tell me if you don't want to—maybe I oughtn't to ask, been so long ago and everything lost track of—but you won't feel offended if I do, will you?" He had his hand on Gregg's shoulder now, his lips quivering, a peculiar look in his eyes. "Come across here with me, please. No—this way, to the fireplace. Where did you get that portrait?"

Gregg felt a sudden relief. The man wasn't drunk—it was the beauty of the picture which had affected him. He could forgive him that, although he felt sure the next move would be an offer to purchase it. He had met his kind before.

"I bought it at private sale," he answered simply.

"When?"

"Yesterday."

"Who sold it to you?"

"Schenck, the auctioneer."

OLD-FASHIONED GENTLEMAN

"Will you sell it to me?"

"No; I never sell anything of that kind."

"Not at a large price?"

"Not any price," Gregg replied in a decided tone. It was just as he expected. These men of business gauge everything by their bank accounts. One of them had had the impertinence to ask him to fill up a blank check for the contents of his studio.

"Where did it come from?"

"Schenck told me he didn't know. It was held for storage. It seems to interest you?" There was a slight tone of resentment in Gregg's voice.

"Yes, it does, more than I can tell you, more than you can understand." His voice had lost its nervousness now.

"It reminds you of some one, perhaps?" asked Gregg. There might, after all, be some spark of sentiment in the young man.

"Yes, it does," he continued, devouring it with his eyes. "I haven't seen it since I was a child."

"You know it, then!" It was Gregg's turn to be surprised. "Where did you see it, may I ask?"

"Down in Maryland, at Derwood Manor, before it was burned."

The blood mounted to Gregg's cheeks and he was about to speak. Then he checked himself. He did not want to know of the portrait's vicissitudes. That it was now where he could be locked up with it, made up for everything it had come through.

"Yes, these memories are very curious," remarked

AN OLD-FASHIONED GENTLEMAN

Gregg in a more gentle tone. "It reminds me also of some one I once knew. Don't you think it is very beautiful?"

"Beautiful! *Beautiful!* It's the most beautiful thing in the world to me! Why, it's my own mother, Mr. Gregg!"

"You—your own mother! What's your name?"

"Philip Colton."

VII

The same poise that restrained Adam Gregg when he came suddenly upon Olivia's portrait in the auction-room sustained him when he looked into the eyes of the young man whom, years before, he had left as a child at Derwood Manor.

"Are you sure?" he asked. He knew he was—he only wanted some fresh light on the dark record. For years the book had been sealed.

"Am I sure? Why it used to be in the garret till my father died, and then my mother brought it down into her room. I have seen her sit before it for hours—she loved it. And once I found her kissing it. Strange, isn't it, how a woman will regret her youth?—and yet I always thought my mother beautiful even when her hair turned gray."

Gregg turned his head and tightened his fingers. For an instant he feared his tears would unman him.

"If it is your mother's portrait," he said, "the picture belongs to you, not to me. I bought it because it recalled a face I once knew, and for its beauty. A man has but one mother, and if your own was like this one she must be your most precious memory. I did not intend to part with it, but I'll give it to you."

"Oh! you are very good, Mr. Gregg," burst out the young man, grasping Adam's hand (Adam caught Olivia's smile now, flashing across his features), "but I have no place for it—not yet. I may have later, when I have a home of my own; that depends upon my business. I'll only ask you to let me come in once in a while to see it."

Gregg returned the grasp heartily, declaring that his door was always open to him at any time and the picture at his disposal whenever he should claim it. He did not tell him he had painted it. He did not tell him that he had known either Olivia or his father, or of his visit ten years later. That part of his life had had a sad and bitter end. Both of them were dead; the house in ruins—why rake among the cinders?

All that spring, in response to Adam's repeated welcomes, Philip Colton made excuses to drop into Gregg's studio. At first to postpone the time for Mr. Eggleston's sittings; then to invite Gregg to dinner at his club to meet some brother financiers, which Gregg declined; again to get his opinion on some trinkets he had bought, and still again to bring him some flowers, he having noticed that the painter was never without them—nor was the portrait, for that matter, Adam always placing a cluster of blossoms or a bunch of roses near the picture, either on the mantel beneath or on the table beside it.

Sometimes Adam when leaving his door on a crack would find that in his absence in an adjoining studio,

OLD-FASHIONED GENTLEMAN

Colton had come and gone, the only record of his visit being a mass of roses he himself had placed beneath his mother's portrait. Once he surprised the young man standing before it looking up into the eyes as if waiting for her to speak. Incidents like these showed his better and more sympathetic nature and drew Adam to him the closer.

And the growth of the friendship was not all on one side. Not only was Gregg's type of man absolutely new to the young financier, but his workshop was a never-ending surprise. The fact that neither bonds nor stocks, nor anything connected with them, was ever discussed inside its tapestried walls, opened up for him new vistas in life. The latest novel might be gone into or a character in a recent play; or the rendering of a symphony, or some fresh discovery in science, but nothing of gain. What struck him as more extraordinary still was the air of repose that was everywhere apparent, so different from his own busy life, and at any hour of the day, too. This was apparent not only in the voices, but in the attitude and bearing of the men who formed the painter's circle of friends.

Sometimes he would find Macklin, the sculptor—up from his atelier in the basement—buried in a chair and a book, pipe in mouth, before Gregg's fire—had been there for hours when Phil entered. Again he would catch the sound of the piano as he mounted the stairs, only to discover Putney, the landscape painter, running his fingers over the keys, while Adam stood before his easel touching his canvas here or there; or he would interrupt old Sonheim, who kept the book-shop at the corner, and who had known Adam for years—while he read aloud this and that quotation from a musty volume, Adam stretched out at full length on his divan, the smoke of his cigarette drifting blue in the overhead light.

These restful contrasts to his own life interested and astonished him. Since his father's death he had had few hours of real repose. While not yet fifteen he had been thrown out into the world to earn his bread. A successful earning, for he was already head of his firm, in which his prospective father-in-law, Mr. Eggleston, the rich banker, was special partner, and young Eggleston the junior member. An honorable career, too, for the house stood high in the Street, and its credit was above reproach in the commercial world, their company—the Portage Copper Company, whose securities they financed—being one of the many important mining properties in the great Northwest. All this he owed to his own indomitable will and pluck, and to his untiring industry—a quality developed in many another young Southerner the victim of the war and its aftermath.

And he was always welcome.

Apart from the tie that bound them together—of which Philip was unconscious—Adam's heart went out to the young fellow as many another childless, wifeless man's has gone out to youth. He loved his enthusiasms, his industry, his successes. Most of all he loved the young man's frankness—the way in which he kept nothing back—even his earlier escapades, many of which he should have been ashamed of. Then again he loved the reverence with which Phil treated him, the deference to his opinions, the acceptance of his standards. Most of all he loved him for the memory of the long ago.

It was only when the overmastering power of money became the dominant force—the one recognized and gloated over by Philip—that his face grew grave. It was then that the older and wiser man, with his keen insight into the human heart, trembled for the younger, fearing that some sudden pressure, either of fortune or misfortune, might sweep him off his feet. It was at these times—Philip's face all excitement with the telling—that Adam's penetrating eyes, searching into the inner places, would find the hard, almost pitiless lines which he remembered so well in the father's face repeated in the son's.

There was, however, one subject which swept these lines out of his face. That was when Phil would speak of Madeleine, the rich banker's daughter—Madeleine with her sunny eyes and merry laugh—"Only up to my shoulder—such a dear girl!" Then there would break over the young man's face that joyous, irradiating smile, that sudden sparkle of the eye and quiver of the lip that had made his own mother's face so enchanting. On these occasions the Street and all it stood for, as well as books and everything else, was forgotten and Madeleine would become the sole topic. These two influences struggled for mastery in the young man's heart; influences unknown to Philip, but clear as print to the eye of the thoughtful man of the world who, day by day, read his companion's mind the clearer.

As to Madeleine no subject could be more congenial.

When a young fellow under thirty has found a sympathetic old fellow of fifty to listen to talks of his sweetheart, and when that old fellow of fifty has found a companion with a look in his eyes of the woman he loved and who carries in his face something of the joy he knew in youth, it is no wonder that these two became still greater friends, or that Philip's tread outside Adam Gregg's door was always followed by a quick beat of the painter's heart and a warm grasp of his hand.

One afternoon Philip came in with a spring quite different from either his nervous walk or his more measured tread—his "bank director's step" Adam used to call it with a smile. This time he was on his toes, his hands in the air tossing the velvet curtains aside with a swing as he sprang inside.

"Madeleine's home from the West!" he burst out. "Now at last you'll see her, and you've got to paint her, too. Oh, she knows all about the portrait and how you found it; and this studio and the blossoms you love, and everything. My letters have been full of nothing else all winter. She's crazy to see you."

"Not any more crazy than I am to see her," laughed Adam, with his hand on the young man's shoulder.

And so one spring morning—all beautiful things

OLD-FASHIONED GENTLEMAN

came to him on spring mornings, Adam told her—Madeleine pushed her pretty little head between the velvet curtains and peered in, Phil close behind her, a bunch of violets in his button-hole.

"This is dear Adam Gregg, Madeleine," was her lover's introduction, "and there's nobody like him, and never will be."

The girl stopped, the overhead light falling on her dainty hat and trim figure; her black eyes in comprehensive glance taking in Adam standing against a hazy background of beautiful things with both hands outstretched.

"And I am so glad to be here and to know you," she said, walking straight towards him and laying her little hands in his.

"And so am I," answered Adam. "And I know everything about you. Phil says you can ride like the wind, and dance so that your toes never touch the floor, and that you——"

"Yes, and so do I know every single thing about you"—here she looked at him critically—"and you—yes, you are just as I hoped you would be. Phil's letters have had nothing else in them since you bewitched him and I've just been wild to get home and have him bring me here. What a lovely place! Isn't it wonderful, Phil? . . . And is that the portrait? Oh! what a beautiful, beautiful woman!"

She had left Gregg now—before he had had time to say another word in praise of her—and was standing under the picture, her eyes gazing into its depths.

Adam kept perfectly still, completely charmed by her dainty joyousness. He felt as if some rare bird had flown in which would be frightened away if he moved a hair's breadth. Phil stood apart watching every expression that crossed her happy face. He had been waiting weeks for this moment.

"You haven't her eyes or her hair, Phil," she continued without turning her head, "but you look at me that way sometimes. I don't know what it is—she's happy, and she's not happy. She loved somebody—that's it, she *loved* somebody and her eyes follow you so—they seem alive—and the lips as if they could speak.

"And now, Mr. Gregg, please show me every one of these beautiful things." She had already, with her quick intuition, seen through Adam's personality at a glance, and found out how thoroughly she could trust him.

He obeyed as gallantly and as cheerfully as if he had been her own age, pulling open the drawers of the cabinets, taking out this curio and that, lifting the lid of the old Venetian wedding-chest that she might herself pry among the velvets and embroideries; she dropping on her knees beside it with all the fluttering joy of a child who had come suddenly upon a box of toys; Phil following them around the room putting in a word here and there, reminding Adam of something he had forgotten, or calling her attention to some object hidden in a shadow that even her quick absorbing glance had overlooked.

OLD-FASHIONED GENTLEMAN

Once more she stopped before the portrait, her eyes drinking in its beauty.

"Don't you love it, Mr. Gregg?"

"Yes, but I'm going to give it to your—to Philip."

"Oh! you know! do you? Yes, just say it out. We *are* going to be married just as soon as we can—next October is the very latest date. I told father we were tired of waiting and he has promised me; we would have been married this spring but for that horrid copper mine that the deeper you go the less copper——"

"Oh, but Madeleine," protested Philip with a sudden flush in his face, "that was some time ago; everything's all right now."

"Well, I don't know much about it; I only repeated what father said."

And then having had her fill of all the pretty things—some she must go back to half a dozen times in her delight—especially some "ducky" little china dogs that were "just too sweet for anything"; and having discussed to her heart's content all the details of the coming wedding—especially the part where Adam was to walk close behind them on their way up the aisle of the church as a sort of fairy godfather to give Phil away—the joyous little bird, followed by the happy young lover, spread her dainty wings and flew away.

And thus it was that two new spirits were added to Adam Gregg's long list of friends: One the young man, earnest, alert, losing no chance in his business, awake to all the changes in the ever-shifting market, conversant with every move of his opponents and meet-

AN OLD-FASHIONED GENTLEMAN

ing them with a shrewdness—and sometimes, Adam thought—with a cunning far beyond his years. The other, the fresh, outspoken, merry young girl, fluttering in and out like a bird in her ever-changing plumage—now in hat loaded with tea-roses, now in trim walking costume fitting her dainty figure; now in her waterproof, her wee little feet "wringing wet" she would tell Adam with a laugh—always a welcome guest, no matter who had his chair, or whose portrait or what work required his brush.

VIII

One afternoon, some days after Philip's return from an inspection of the mines of the Portage Copper Company, and an hour ahead of his usual time, the velvet curtain was pushed aside and the young man walked in. Not only did he move with his most important "bank director's step," but he brought with him an air of responsibility only seen in magnates who control the destinies of corporations and the savings of their stockholders.

"What's the matter, Phil?" asked Adam with a laugh. "Have they made you president of the Stock Exchange, or has the Government turned over its deposits to your keeping, or has the wedding-day been set for to-morrow?"

"Wedding-day's all right; closer than ever, but I've got something that knocks being president of the Exchange cold. Our scheme is about fixed up and it's to be floated next week—float anything on this market—that's better than being president or anything else. Our attorneys brought in the papers this morning, and they will be signed at our office to-morrow at eleven-thirty. The Seaboard Trust Company are going to take half the bonds and two out-of-town banks the balance. That puts us on our legs and keeps us there, and I don't mind telling you"—and he looked around as if fearing to be overhead—"we've got to have this money or— Well, there's no use of my going into that, because it's all over now, or will be when this loan's floated. But I want to tell you that we've had some pretty tough sledding lately—some that the old man doesn't know about."

Adam looked up; any danger that threatened Phil always enlisted his sympathy.

"Tell me about it. I can't follow these operations. Most of them are all Greek to me."

"Well, as I say, we've got to have money, a whole lot of it, or there's no telling when Madeleine and I will ever be married. And the Portage Company has got to have money; they have struck bottom so far as their finances go and can't go on without help. God knows I've worked hard enough over it—been doing nothing else for weeks."

"What do you float?" Adam was prepared to give him his best attention.

"One million refunding bonds—half to take up the old issue and the balance for improvements. Our wedding comes in the 'improvements,'" and Philip winked meaningly.

"Is there enough copper in the mine to warrant the issue?" Adam asked, recalling Madeleine's remark about the deeper they went the less copper there was in the mine.

"What's that got to do with it?"

OLD-FASHIONED GENTLEMAN

"Everything, I should think. You examined it—didn't you?—and should know."

"Yes, but nobody has asked me for an opinion. The company's engineer attends to that."

"What do you think yourself, Phil?"

"I don't think. I'm not paid to think. The other fellow does the thinking and I do the selling."

"What does Mr. Eggleston say?"

"He doesn't say. He isn't paid for saying. What he wants is his six per cent, and that's what we've got to earn. This new deal earns it."

"Does the trust company know anything about the mine?"

"Why, of course, everything. Those fellows don't need a guardian. They've got the mining engineer's sworn certificate, and they trust to that and——"

"And to the standing of your house," Adam interrupted.

"Certainly. Why not? That's what we're in business for."

"But what do you think of it—you, remember; you—Philip Colton—are you willing to swear that the mine is worth the money the trust company will lend on it?"

"I make an affidavit! Not much! What I *say* is everybody's property; what I *think* is nobody's business but my own. The mine *may* strike virgin copper in chunks and it may not. That's where the gamble comes in. If it does the bonus stock they get for nothing will be worth par." He was a little ashamed as he said it. He was merely repeating what he had told his customers in advance of the issue, but they had not returned his gaze with Adam's eyes.

"But you in your heart, Phil, are convinced that it will *not* strike virgin copper, aren't you? So much so that you wouldn't take Madeleine's money, or my money, to put into it." These search-lights of Gregg's had a way of uncovering many secret places.

Philip turned in his chair and looked at Adam. What was the matter with the dear fellow this afternoon, he said to himself.

"Certainly not—and for two reasons: first, you are not in the Street; and second, because I never gamble with a friend's money."

"But you gamble with the money of the innocent men and women who believe in your firm, and who in the end buy these bonds of the trust company, don't you?"

"Well, but what have we got to do with the bonds after we sell them? We are not running the mine, we're only getting money for them to run it on, and incidentally our commissions," and he smiled knowingly. "The trust company does the same thing. This widow-and-orphan business is about played out in the Street. The shrewdest buyers we have are just these people, and they get their cent per cent every time. Don't you bother your dear old head over this matter; just be glad it's coming out all right—I am, I tell you!"

Gregg had risen from his chair and was standing over Philip with a troubled look on his face.

OLD-FASHIONED GENTLEMAN

"Phil," he said slowly, "look at me. From what you tell me, you can't issue these bonds! You can't afford to do it—no honest man can!"

The young financier lay back in his chair and broke out into laughter.

"Old Gentleman," he said, as he reached up his hand and laid it affectionately on Gregg's waistcoat—it was a pet name of his—"you just stick to your brushes and paints and I'll stick to my commissions. If everybody in the Street had such old-fashioned notions as you have we'd starve to death. We've got to take risks, everybody has. You might as well say that when a stock is going up and against us we shouldn't cover right away to save ourselves from further loss; or that when it's going down we shouldn't sell and saddle the other fellow with the slump while we get from under. Now I'm going home to tell Madeleine the good news; she's been on pins and needles for a week."

Gregg began pacing the floor, his hands behind his back. His movements were so unusual and his face bore so troubled a look that Philip, who had thrown away his cigar and had picked up his hat preparatory to leaving the room, delayed his departure.

Adam halted in front of him and now stood gazing into his face, an expression on his own that showed the younger man how keenly he had taken the refusal.

"I know I'm old-fashioned, Phil—I have a right to be. I come of old-fashioned stock—so do you. All that you tell me of your father convinces me that he was an upright man. He was severe at times, and dominating, but he was honest. Your mother's purity and goodness shine out here," and he pointed to the portrait. "This is your heritage, and your only heritage—something that millions of money cannot buy, and which you cannot sell, no matter what price is paid you for it. You, their son"—Gregg stopped and hesitated, the words seemed to clog in his throat—"must not—*shall not!*" (the way was clear now) "commit a crime which would bring a blush to their cheeks if they were alive to-day. Dont, I beseech you, my boy, lend your young manhood to this swindle. It is infamous, it is damnable. It shall not—*cannot* be. You love me too well to refuse; promise me you will stop this whole business."

Colton was astounded. In all his intercourse with Gregg he had never seen him moved like this. He knew what had caused it. Gregg's sedentary life, his being so much away from the business side of things had warped his judgment and upset his reasoning powers. Not to make commissions on a loan that the first mining expert in the country had declared good, and which the biggest trust company in the Street and two outside banks were willing to underwrite! Gregg was crazy! This came of talking business to such a man. He should have confined himself to more restful topics—topics which he really loved best. After all, it was his fault, not Adam's.

"All right, old fellow; don't let us talk any more about it," he said in the tone he would have used to

"Promise me that you will stop the whole business."

OLD-FASHIONED GENTLEMAN

pacify a woman who had lost her temper. "Some other time when——"

Adam resumed his walk without listening further. He saw how futile had been his appeal and the thought alarmed him all the more.

"Put down your hat, Phil." The calmness of his voice was singularly in contrast to the tone of the outburst. "Take your seat again. Wait until I lock the door. I have something to say to you and we must not be interrupted."

He turned the key, drew the heavy curtains together, and dragging his chair opposite Phil's so that he could look squarely in his eyes, sat down in front of him.

"My son," he began, "I am going to tell you something which has been locked in my own heart ever since you were a boy of five. Something I have never told you before because it only brought sorrow and suffering to me, and I wanted only the sunny side of life for you and Madeleine, and so I have kept still. I tell you now in the hope that it may save you from an act you will never cease to regret.

"There comes a time in every man's life when he meets the fork in the road. This is his crisis. One path leads to destruction, the other, perhaps, to misery —but a misery in which he can still look every man in the face and his God as well. You have reached it. You may not think so, but you have. Carry out what you have told me and you are no longer an honest man. Don't be offended. Listen and don't interrupt me. Nothing you could say to me would hurt my

heart; nothing I shall say to you should hurt yours.
I love you with a love you know not of. I loved you
when you were no higher than my knee."

Phil looked at him in amazement, and was about to
speak when Adam waved his hand.

"No, don't speak. Hear me until I have finished.
Only to save the boy she loved would I lay bare my
heart as I am going to do to you now. Turn your
head! Do you see that picture? I painted it some
twenty-five years ago; you were a child then, five
years old. I was younger than you are now; full of
my art; full of the promise of life. Your father's
home was a revelation to me: the comfort of it, the
servants, the luxury, the warm welcome he gave me,
the way he treated me, not as a stranger, but as a son.
A few days after I arrived he left me in charge of his
home. Your mother was three years younger than I
was; you were a little fellow tugging at her skirts.

"The four weeks that followed, while your father
was away and I was painting the portrait, were to me a
dream. At the end of it I awoke in torment. I had
reached the fork in my road: one path lay to perdition,
the other to a suffering that has followed me all my life.
Your father was an austere man of about my own age
now; it was not a happy union—it was as if Madeleine
and I should be married. Your mother, girl as she
was, respected and honored him and had no other
thought except her duty; I saw it and tried to comfort
her. The day of your father's return home he came
up into the garret which had been turned into a studio

OLD-FASHIONED GENTLEMAN

to see the portrait. The scene that followed has always been to me a horror. He denounced her and me. He even went so far as to say the picture was immodest because of the gown, and in his anger turned it to the wall. You can see for yourself how unjust was that criticism. He found out he was wrong and said so afterward, but it did not heal the wound. Your mother was crushed and outraged.

"That night she came up to the studio and poured out her heart to me. I won't go over it—I cannot. There was in her eyes something that frightened me. Then my own were opened. Down in front of me lay an abyss; around it were the two paths. All night I paced the floor; I laid my soul bare; I pleaded; I argued with myself. I reasoned it out with God; I urged her unhappiness—the difference in their ages; the harshness of the older man; her patient submission. Then there rose up before me the sterner law— my own responsibility; the trust placed in my hands; her youth, my youth. Gradually the mist in my mind cleared and I saw the path ahead. There was but one road: that I must take!

"When the dawn broke I lifted the portrait from where your father had placed it with its face against the wall; kissed it with all the reverence a boy's soul could have for his ideal, crept down the stairs, saddled my horse and rode away.

"Ten years later—after your father's death—I again went to Derwood Manor—in the autumn—in November. I wanted to look into her face once more—even before I looked into my own father's—to see the brook we loved, the hills we wandered over, the porch where we sat and talked. I had heard nothing of the house being in ruins, or of your mother's death. Everything was gone! Everything—everything!"

Adam rested his head in his hands, his fingers shielding his eyes. Philip sat looking at him in silence, his face torn with conflicting emotions—astonishment, sympathy, an intense love for the man predominating. Adam continued, the words coming in half-muffled tones, from behind his hands, as if he were talking to himself, with now and then a pause.

"You wonder, Phil, why I live alone this way—you often ask me that question. Do you know why? It is because I have never been able to love any other woman. She set a standard for me that no other woman has ever filled. All my young life was bound up in her long after I left her. For years I thought of nothing else; my only hope was in keeping away. I would not be responsible for myself or for her if we ever met again. She wasn't mine; she was your father's. She couldn't be mine as long as he was alive."

He raised his head and resumed his old position, his voice rising, his earnest, determined manner dominating his words.

"I ask you now, Phil, what would have become of you if I had left that stain upon his name and upon yours? Who brought me to myself? She did! How? By her confidence in me; that gave me my

OLD-FASHIONED GENTLEMAN

strength. I knew that night, as well as I know that I am sitting here, that we could not go on the way we had been going with safety. I knew also that it all rested with me. For me to unsettle her love for your father during his lifetime would have been damnable. Only one thing was left—flight— That I took and that you must take. Turn your eyes, Phil, and look at her. She saved me from myself; she will save you from yourself. Do you suppose that anything but purity, goodness, and truth ever came from out those lips? Do you think she would be satisfied with anything else in her boy? Be a man, my son! Strangle this temptation that threatens to stain your soul. No matter what comes—even if you beg your bread—put this thing under your feet. Look your God in the face!"

During the long recital Phil's mind had gone back to his childhood's days in confirmation of the strange story. As Adam talked on, his eyes flashing, his voice tremulous with the pathos of the story he was pouring into the young man's astonished ears, one picture after another rose dimly out of the listener's past: The big lounge in the garret where his mother held him in her arms; the high window with the light flooding the floor of the room; the jar of blossoms into which he had thrust his little face.

He did not move when Adam finished, nor for some minutes did he speak. At last he said in a voice that showed how deeply he had been stirred:

"It's all true. It all comes back to me now. I

must have been too young to remember you, but I remember the picture. I looked for it everywhere after she died, but I couldn't find it. Then came the fire and everything was swept away. Some one must have stolen it while we were in Baltimore. And you have loved my mother all these years, Gregg, and never told me?"

He was on his feet now and had his arm around Adam's shoulder. "Couldn't you trust me, Old Gentleman? Don't you know how close you are to me? Did you think I wouldn't understand? What you tell me about your leaving her is no surprise. You wouldn't—you couldn't do anything else. That's because you are a man and a gentleman. You are doing such things every day of your life; that's why everybody loves you. As to what you want me to do, don't say any more to me"—the tears he was hiding were choking him. "Let me go home. What you have told me of my mother, of yourself—everything has knocked me out. My judgment has gone—I must think it all over. I know every word you have said about the loan is true; but I haven't told you all. The situation is worse than you think. Everything depends on it—Madeleine—her father—all of us. If I could have found some other plan—if you had only talked to me this way before. But I've promised them all—they expect it. No! Don't speak to me. Don't say another word. Let me go home." And he flung himself from the room.

Adam sat still. The confession had wrung his soul;

OLD-FASHIONED GENTLEMAN

the pain seemed unbearable. What the outcome would be God only knew. With a quick movement, as if seeking relief, he rose to his feet and walked to the portrait. Then lifting his hands above his head with the movement of a despairing suppliant before the Madonna he cried out:

"Help him, my beloved. Help him as you did me."

IX

At the offices of Philip Colton & Co., just off Wall Street, an unusual stir was apparent—an air of expectancy seemed to pervade everything. The cashier had arrived at his desk half an hour earlier than usual, and so had the stock clerk and the two book-keepers. This had been in accordance with Mr. Colton's instructions the night before, and they had been carried out to the minute. The papers in the big copper loan, he had told the stock clerk, were to be signed at half-past eleven o'clock the next morning, and he wanted all the business of the preceding day cleaned up and out of the way before the new deal went through. This accomplished, he said to himself, Mr. Eggleston would be able to retire a part if not all of his special capital, and his dear Madeleine, to quote a morning journal, find a place by the side of "one of the bright young financiers of our time."

Mr. Eggleston, in tan-colored waistcoat, white gaiters and shiny silk hat, a gold-headed cane in one hand—the embodiment of a prosperous man of affairs—also arrived half an hour earlier—ten o'clock, really, an event that caused some astonishment, for not twice in the whole year had the special partner reached his son's office so early in the day.

AN OLD-FASHIONED GENTLEMAN

Young Eggleston reached his desk a few minutes after his father. His dress was as costly as his progenitor's, but a trifle more insistent. The waistcoat was speckled with red; the scarf a brilliant scarlet decorated with a horseshoe set in diamonds, and the shoes patent leather. He was one size smaller than his father and had one-tenth of his brains. With regard to every other measurement, however, there was not the slightest doubt but that in a few years he would equal his distinguished father's outlines, a fact already discernible in his middle distance. In looking around for the missing nine-tenths of gray matter his father had found it under Philip Colton's hat, and the formation of the firm, with himself as special and his son as junior, had been the result.

At half-past ten Mr. Eggleston began to be nervous. Every now and then he would walk out into the main office, interview one of the clerks as to his knowledge of Phil's whereabouts and return again to his private office, where he occupied himself drumming on the desk with the end of his gold pencil, and watching the clock. The junior had no such misgivings—none of any kind. He had a game of polo that afternoon at three, and was chiefly concerned lest the day's work might intervene. The signing of similar papers had once kept him at the office until five.

At eleven o'clock a messenger with a bank-book fastened to his waist by a steel chain, brought a message. "The treasurer of the Seaboard, with the company's attorney, would be at Mr. Eggleston's office," the message read, "in half an hour, to sign the papers. Would he be sure to have Mr. Philip Colton present." (The special's social and financial position earned him this courtesy; most of the other magnates had to go to the trust company to culminate such transactions.)

The character of the message and Philip's continued delay only increased Mr. Eggleston's uneasiness. The stock clerk was called in, as well as one of the bookkeepers. "What word, if any, had Mr. Colton given the night before?" he asked impatiently. "What hour did he leave the office? Did any one know of any business which could have detained him? had any telegram been received and mislaid?"—the sum of the replies being that neither word, letter nor telegram had been received, to which was added the proffered information that judging from Mr. Colton's instructions the night before that gentleman must certainly be ill or he would have "showed up" before this.

A few minutes before half-past eleven the treasurer and his attorney were shown into the firm's office, the former a man of sixty, with a cold, smooth-shaven face, ferret eyes and thin, straight lips, thin as the edges of a tight-shut clam, and as bloodless. He was dressed in black and wore a white necktie which gave him a certain ministerial air. His companion, the attorney, was younger and warmer looking, and a trifle stouter, with bushy gray locks under his hat brim, and bushy gray side-whiskers under two red ears that lay flat against his head. He was anything but ministerial, either in deportment or language. What he didn't

OLD-FASHIONED GENTLEMAN

know about corporation law wouldn't have been of the slightest value to anybody—not even to a would-be attorney passing an examination. Both men were short in their speech and incisively polite, with a quick step-in and step-out air about them which showed how thoroughly they had been trained in the school of Street courtesy—the wasting of a minute of each other's valuable time being the unpardonable sin.

"Glad to see you, Mr. Eggleston," exclaimed the treasurer, with one finger extended, into which the special hooked his own. The official did not see the junior partner; he dealt only with principals.

"Our attorney," he continued, nodding to his companion, "has got the papers. Are you all ready? Where is Mr. Colton?" and he looked around.

"I'm expecting him every minute," replied the special in a nervous tone; "but we can get along without him. My son is here to sign for the firm."

"No, we can't get along. I want him. I have some questions to ask him; these are President Stockton's directions."

Before Eggleston could reply the door of the private office was thrust open and Philip stepped in.

Mr. Eggleston sprang from his chair, and a combination smile showing urbanity, apology, and contentment, now that Phil had arrived, overspread his features.

"We had begun to think you were ill, Colton," he said in a relieved tone. "Anything the matter?"

"No, I stopped to see Mr. Gregg. I am on time, I

believe, gentlemen, half-past eleven, wasn't it?" and he consulted his watch. There was a peculiar tremor in Phil's voice that made his prospective father-in-law fasten his eyes upon him as if to learn the cause. Colton looked as if he had been awake all night; he was pale, but otherwise he was himself.

"Yes, you are on the minute," exclaimed the treasurer, picking up the bundle of papers and loosening the tape that bound them together. "You have just returned from the property, we hear. What do you think of it?"

"We have the certificate of the mining engineer," interrupted Mr. Eggleston in a bland tone, regaining his seat.

"Yes, I have it here," the treasurer answered, tapping the bundle of papers. "It is your personal opinion, Mr. Colton, that we want. The president insists upon this; he has a reason for it."

Colton stepped nearer and looked the treasurer square in the eyes.

"My personal opinion, sir," he answered in clear-cut tones, "is that the deposit is practically exhausted. I came here to tell you so. The engineer's report is, I think, too highly colored."

Both father and son started forward in their chairs, their eyes glaring at Philip. They could hardly believe their senses.

"What!" burst out Mr. Eggleston—"you don't mean to say that——"

"One moment, please," interrupted the treasurer,

with an impatient wave of his hand towards Eggleston:
"Do you think, Mr. Colton, that the issue had better be deferred?"

"I do. Certainly until the mine makes a better showing."

Again Mr. Eggleston tried to interrupt and again he was waved into silence.

"When did you arrive at this conclusion?"

"This morning. I thought differently yesterday, but I have changed my mind. So much so that it would be impossible for me to go on with this loan."

"Shall I take that message to the president?"

"Yes. If I have any cause to change my opinion I'll let him know. But it is not likely I will—I'm sorry to have given you all this trouble."

"Thank you," said the trust company's representative, rising from his chair and extending his hand to Philip. "I might as well tell you that we have heard similar reports and our president felt sure that you would give him the facts. He has great confidence in you, Mr. Colton. If he authorizes me to sign the papers after what you have said to me I'll be back here in a few moments. Good-day, sir!" and with a grim smile lighting his face, the treasurer nodded himself out.

Eggleston waited until the trust company's attorney had gathered up his papers and had closed the door behind him—a mere matter of routine with him; almost every day a transaction of this kind was either deferred or culminated—then he swung himself around in his revolving chair, his cheeks purple with rage, and faced Philip.

"Well, sir! what do you think of the mess you've made of this morning's business! Do you for one instant suppose that Stockton will go on with this deal after what you have told him?"

"If he did, sir, it would not be with my consent," answered Philip coldly.

"Your consent! *Your consent!* What do you know about it? Did you ever mine a pound of copper in your life? Did you ever see a pound mined until you made this last trip? And yet you have the effrontery to set yourself up as an expert against one of the best men in his profession! Do you not know that you have made not only the firm but me ridiculous, by your stupid vacillation—and with the Seaboard, of all trust companies! Why didn't you find out all this before you brought these people down here?"

"It is never too late to be honest, sir."

"What do you mean by that!" snapped Eggleston.

"I mean just what I say." Philip's voice was without a tremor, low, forceful and decisive. "The floating of these bonds on the present condition of the mines would have been a fraud. I didn't see it in that way at first, but I do see it now. It is done every day in the Street, I grant you, but it will never be done again with my consent so long as I am a member of this firm!"

Eggleston's lip curled. "You seem to have grown singularly honest overnight, Mr. Colton," he sneered.

OLD-FASHIONED GENTLEMAN

"According to your ideas Bates, Rankin & Co. were frauds when they floated the Imperial, and so were Porter & King when they sold out the Morningside for two millions of dollars."

"None of them are paying, sir, and it was dishonorable to float the bonds." He was still on his feet, facing his prospective father-in-law, holding him at bay really.

"What's that got to do with it?" snarled Eggleston. "They will pay sometime. As to your honor: That's the cheap sentiment you Southern men are always shouting. Your kind of honor won't hold water here! It was your honor when you tried to hold on to your niggers; and it's your honor when you murder each other in duels, and——"

"Stop, Mr. Eggleston!" said Philip, his face white as chalk, every muscle in his body taut—"this has gone far enough. No position that you hold towards me gives you the right to speak as you have. I have done what was right. I could not have looked either you or Madeleine in the face if I had done differently."

Here the door was swung back, cutting short Eggleston's reply, and a note was passed in, the clerk making a hurried inspection of the faces of his employers, as if to learn the cause of the disturbance.

Eggleston read it and handed it to his son, who so far had not opened his mouth. He could reach the game in time, anyhow.

"Just as I expected!" hissed Eggleston between his teeth: "'Must decline the loan,' he says. 'Thank Mr. Colton for his frankness. Stockton, President.'

Thanks Mr. Colton, does he! If you want my opinion I'll tell you that by your confounded backing and filling you've thrown over the best operation we've had since this firm was formed. Find the money somewhere else, Mr. Colton, that I've put in, and I'll draw out. This morning's work convinces me that no sensible man's interests are safe in your hands."

"That will be difficult, sir, when the condition of our firm is known, as it must be. Furthermore, it would be impossible for me to ask it. Since I've been here I've done my best to look after your interests. Some of our ventures, I regret to say, have been unsuccessful. Instead of releasing your capital I shall need some fifty thousand dollars more to carry us through. The situation is upon us and I might as well discuss it with you now."

"We don't owe a dollar we can't pay," blurted out Eggleston, picking up his hat and cane.

"That is true to-day, but to-morrow it may not be. The refusal of this loan by the Seaboard will send back to us every copper stock we have borrowed money on. They are good, better than Portage, but the banks won't believe it. I want this additional money to tide this over."

"You won't get a dollar!"

"Then I'll notify the Exchange of our suspension at once. If we stop now we can carry out your statement and pay every dollar we owe. If we keep on with the market as it is we may not pay fifty cents. Which will you do?"

OLD-FASHIONED GENTLEMAN

"Not a dime, sir! Not a cent! Do you hear me—not one cent! You two fools can work it out to suit yourselves. I'm through with you both!" and he slammed the door behind him.

The boys were already crying the news of the downfall of his house when, late that afternoon, Philip pushed aside the velvet curtain and stepped into Adam's studio. He had bought an extra on his way uptown and held it in his hand. "Failure in Wall Street! Philip Colton & Co. suspend!" the headlines read.

"It's all over, Gregg," he said, dropping into a chair, without even offering the painter his hand.

"And he refused to help!" exclaimed Adam.

"Yes, not a cent! There was nothing else to do. We can pay every dollar we owe, but it leaves me stranded. Madeleine is the worst part of it. I did not think she'd go back on me. They are furious at her house. I stopped there, but she wouldn't see me—nobody would. She's wrong, and when she gets the truth she'll think differently, but it's pretty hard while it lasts."

Adam laid his hand on Phil's shoulder and looked steadily into his face.

"Do you regret it, Phil?" The old search-lights were sweeping right and left again.

"Yes, all the trouble it brings and the injury to the firm and to Mr. Eggleston, for I don't forget he's my partner. I didn't think it would end in ruin. I bungled it badly, maybe."

"Are you sorry?"

"No, I'd do it over again!" answered Philip firmly, as he glanced at the portrait.

Gregg tightened his grasp on Philip's shoulder. "That's the true ring, my son!" he cried, his eyes filling with tears. "I've never loved you as I do this minute Now you begin to live. This day marks the parting. of the roads: From this day you go forward, not back. It doesn't make any difference what happens or what things you——"

"And you don't think Madeleine will——"

"Think Madeleine will lose her love for you! You don't know the girl—not for one minute. Of course, everything is upside down, and of course there'll be bad blood. Mr. Eggleston is angry, but he'll get over it. What he has lost to-day he has made a dozen times over in his career in a single turn in stocks, and will again. Keep your head up! Finish your work at the office; pay every cent you owe; come back here and let me know if anything is left, and then we'll see Madeleine. You'll find my check-book in that desk at your elbow. I'll sign as many checks in blank as you want and you can fill them up at your leisure. We'll fight this thing out together and we'll win. Madeleine stop loving you! I'll stake my head she won't!"

Events move with great rapidity in the Street. When a tin case the size of a candle-box can be brought in by two men and a million of property dumped out on a table, an immediate accounting of assets is not difficult.

OLD-FASHIONED GENTLEMAN

Once their value is fixed by the referee they can be dealt to those interested as easily as a pack of cards.

By noon of the following day not only did the firm of Philip Colton & Co. know exactly where they stood, but so did every one of the firm's creditors: Seventy per cent cash and thirty per cent in sixty days was the settlement. All their outside stocks had been closed out under the rule. Philip's thorough business methods and the simplicity and clearness with which his books had been kept made such an adjustment not only possible, but easy. The net result was the wiping out of the special capital of Philip's prospective father-in-law and all of his own capital and earnings. The junior partner was not affected; his allowance went on as usual. He did not even sell his stud; he bought another pony. His father gave him the money; it helped the family credit.

So far not a word had come from Madeleine. Philip had rung the bell of the Eggleston mansion three times since that fatal morning and had been told by the butler in frigid tones that Miss Eggleston "was not at home." None of his notes were answered. That so sensible a girl as Madeleine, one whose whole nature was frankness and love, could be so cruel and so unjust was a disappointment more bitter than the failure.

"She has been lied to by somebody," broke out Philip as he paced up and down Adam's studio, "or she is locked up where nothing can reach her. All my notes come back unopened; the last redirected by Mr.

Eggleston himself. Neither he nor his son has been to the office since the settlement. They leave me to sweep up after them—dirty piece of business. Will there be any use in your seeing Mr. Eggleston?"

Adam looked into space for a moment.

He had never met the senior. He had, out of deference to Phil, and contrary to his habitual custom, given him preference over his other sitters, but Eggleston had not kept his appointment and Gregg had postponed the painting of the portrait until the following season. Phil had made excuses, but Adam had only smiled and with the remark—"Time enough next winter," had changed the subject.

"No. Let a young girl manage her own affairs," Adam answered in a decided tone, "especially a girl like Madeleine." He had seen too much misery from interfering with a young girl's heart.

"What do you advise then?"

"To let the storm blow over," Adam replied firmly.

"But you've said that for a week and I am no better off. I can't stand it much longer, Old Gentleman. I *must* see Madeleine, I tell you. What can you do to help? Now—not to-morrow or next week?"

"Nothing that would be wise."

"But you promised me to go and see her the afternoon we went to smash."

"So I did, and I'll go if you wish me to."

"When?"

"To-morrow morning. It is against my judgment to do anything until you hear from her. A woman al-

OLD-FASHIONED GENTLEMAN

ways finds the way. Madeleine is no exception. She loves you too well not to. But I'll go, my boy, and try."

"You *must* go. I tell you I can't and won't wait. I have done nothing I'm ashamed of. Our wedding is off, of course, until I can look around and see what I'm going to do, but that's no reason why we can't continue to see each other."

The butler met him with a polite but decided: "Miss Eggleston is not receiving."

"Take her that card," said Gregg. "I'll wait here for an answer."

The erect figure of the painter, his perfect address, coupled with the air of command which always seemed a part of him, produced an instantaneous curve in the butler's spine.

"Step into the library, sir," he said in a softer tone as he pushed aside the heavy portières for Adam to enter.

Gregg entered the curtain-muffled room with its marble statues, huge Sèvres vases and ponderous gold frames, swept a glance over the blue satin sofas and cumbersome chairs in the hope of finding Madeleine curled up somewhere among the heap of cushions, and then, hat in hand, took up his position in front of the cheerless, freshly varnished hearth to await that young lady's coming. What he would say or how he would approach the subject nearest to his heart would depend on her mental attitude. That she loved Phil as dearly as he loved her there was no question. That she had begun to suffer for loss of him was equally sure. A leaf from his own past told him that.

Again the butler's step was heard in the hall; there came a sound of an opening door, and Mr. Eggleston entered.

As he approached the dealer's description of his white hair and red face—a subject Franz Hal would have loved—came back to the painter.

Adam advanced to meet him with that perfect poise which distinguished him in surprises of this kind.

"Mr. Eggleston, is it not?"

"Yes, and whom have I the pleasure of addressing?" —glancing at the card in his hand.

"I am Adam Gregg. We were to meet some time ago, when I was to paint your portrait. This time I came to see your daughter Madeleine."

Mr. Eggleston's manner dropped thermometer-like from the summer heat of graciousness to the zero of reserve: the portrait was no longer a pleasant topic. Moreover he had always believed that the painter had advised Philip the morning of his "asinine declination" of the trust company's proposition.

"May I ask what for?" It was a brutal way of putting it, but the banker had a brutal way of putting things. Generally he confounded the person before him with the business discussed, venting upon him all his displeasure.

"To try and have her receive Philip Colton, or at least to get her reason for not doing so. It may be that

OLD-FASHIONED GENTLEMAN

it is due to your own objection; if so I should like to talk the matter over with you."

"You are quite right, sir; I do object—object in the strongest manner. I don't wish him here. I've had all I want of Mr. Colton, and so has my daughter."

"May I ask why?"

"I don't know that it is necessary for me to discuss it with you, Mr. Gregg."

"I am his closest friend, and have known him ever since he was five years old."

"Then I positively decline to discuss it with you, sir, for I should certainly say something that would wound your feelings. It is purely a matter of business, and that you artists never understand. If you will excuse me I will return to Mrs. Eggleston; she is an invalid, as you have no doubt heard, and I spend the morning hour with her. I must ask you to excuse me, sir."

On his return to his studio Gregg began to pace the floor, his habit when anything worried him. Phil was to return at three o'clock and he had nothing but bad news for him. That his visit had only made matters worse was too evident. Never in all his life had he been treated with such discourtesy. Eggleston was a vulgarian and a brute, but he was Madeleine's father, and he could not encourage her to defy him. He, of course, wanted these two young people to meet, but not in any clandestine way. Her father, no doubt, would soon see things differently, for success was the foot-rule by which he measured a man, and Phil, with his energy and honesty, would gain this in time. Phil must wait. Everything would come right once the boy got on his legs again. The failure had in every way been an honest one. In this connection he recalled the remark of a visitor who had dropped into the studio the day before and who in discussing the failure had said in the crisp vernacular of the Street: "Bitten off more than they could chew, but square as a brick." It was an expression new to him but he had caught its meaning. That his fellow-brokers had this opinion of Philip meant half the battle won. Men who by a lift of their fingers lose or make fortunes in a din that drowns their voices, and who never lie or crawl, no matter what the consequences, have only contempt for a man who hides his wallet. "Hands out and everything you've got on the table," is their creed. This done their pockets are wide open and every hand raised to help the other fellow to his feet.

All these thoughts raced through Adam's head as he continued to pace the floor. Now and then he would stop in his walk and look intently at some figure in the costly rug beneath his feet, as if the solution of his problem lay in its richly colored surface. Two questions recurred again and again: What could he do to help? and how could he get hold of Madeleine?

As the hours wore on he became more restless. Early that morning—before he had gone to Madeleine's—his brush, spurred by his hopes, had worked as if it had been inspired. Not only had the sitter's

OLD-FASHIONED GENTLEMAN

head been blocked in with masterly strokes, but with such fulness and power that few of them need ever be retouched—a part of his heart, in fact, had gone into the blending of every flesh tone. But it was all over now; his enthusiasm and sureness had fled. In fact, he had, on his return, dropped his brushes into his ginger-jar for his servant to clean, and given up painting for the day.

Soon he began fussing about his studio, looking over a portfolio for a pose he needed; replacing some books in his library; adding fresh water to the roses that stood under Olivia's portrait—gazing up into its eyes as if some help could be found in their depths—his uneasiness increasing every moment as the hour of Phil's return approached.

At the sound of a quick step in the corridor—how well he knew the young man's tread—he threw open the door and pushed aside the velvet curtain. Better welcome the poor fellow with a smile and a cheery word.

"Come in, Phil!" he cried—"Come—*Why, Madeleine!*"

She stood just outside the door, a heavy brown veil tied over her hat, her trim figure half concealed by a long cloak. For an instant she did not speak, nor did she move.

"Yes, it's I, Mr. Gregg," she sobbed. "Are you sure there's nobody with you? Oh, I'm so wretched! I had to come: Please let me talk to you. Father told me you had been to see me. He was furious when you went away, and I know how he must have behaved to you." She seemed completely prostrated. Buoyant temperaments pendulate in extremes.

He had drawn her inside now, his arms about her, holding her erect as he led her to a seat with the same tenderness of voice and manner he would have shown his own daughter.

"You poor, dear child!" he cried at last. "Now tell me about it. You know how I love you both."

"Oh, Mr. Gregg, it is so dreadful!" she moaned in piteous tone as she sank upon the cushions of the divan, Adam sitting beside her, her hand tight clasped in his own. "I didn't think Phil would bring all this trouble on us. I would forgive him anything but the way in which he deceived papa. He knew there was no copper in the mine, and he kept saying there was, and went right on speculating and using up everything they had, and then when it was all to be found out he turned coward and ruined everybody—and broke my heart! Oh, the cruel—cruel—" and again she hid her face in the cushions.

"What would you think, little girl, if I told you that I advised him to do it?" he pleaded as he patted her shoulder to quiet her.

"You couldn't do it!" Madeleine burst out in an incredulous tone, raising herself on her elbow to look the better into his eyes. "You *wouldn't* do it! You are too kind."

"But I did—as much for your sake and your father's and brother's as for his own. All the firm has lost so

OLD-FASHIONED GENTLEMAN

far is money. That can be replaced. Had Philip not told the truth it would have been their honor. That could never have been replaced."

And then with her hands fast in his, every thought that crossed her mind revealed in her sweet, girlish face, Adam, his big, frank, brown eyes looking into hers, told her the story of Philip's resolve. Not the part which the portrait had played—not one word of that. She would not have understood; then, too, that was Phil's secret, not his, to tell; but the awakening of the dormant nature of an honest man, incrusted with precedents and half-strangled in financial sophistries, to the truth of what lay about him.

"You wouldn't want his lips to touch yours, my child, if they were stained with a lie; nor could you have worn your wedding-gown if the money that paid for it had been stolen. Your father will see it in the same light some day. Then, if he had a dozen daughters he would give every one of them to men like Philip Colton. The boy wants your help now; he is without a penny in the world and has all his life to begin over again. Now he can begin it clean. Get your arms around his neck and tell him you love him and trust him. He needs you more to-day than he will ever need you in all his life."

She had crept closer to him, nestling under his big shoulders. It seemed good to touch him. Somehow there radiated from this man a strength and tenderness which she had never known before: In the tones of his voice, in the feel of his hand, in the restfulness that pervaded his every word and gesture. For the first time, it seemed to her, she realized what it was to have a father.

"And won't you talk to papa again, Mr. Gregg?" she pleaded in a more hopeful voice.

"Yes, if you wish me to, but it would do no good—not now. It is not your father this time, it's you. Will you help Phil make the fight, little girl? You love him, don't you?"

"Oh, with all my heart!"

"Well, then, tell him so. He will be here in a few minutes."

Madeleine sprang from her seat:

"No, I must not see him," she cried in frightened tones; "I promised my father. I came at this time because I knew he would not be here. Let me go: We are having trouble enough. No—please, Mr. Gregg—no, I must go."

"And what shall I tell Phil?" He dared not persuade her.

"Tell him—tell him—Oh, Mr. Gregg, you know how I love him!"

She was through the curtains and halfway down the corridor before he could reach the door. All the light had come back to her eyes and the spring to her step.

Adam walked to the banisters and listened to the patter of her little feet descending the stairs to the street. Then he went back into the studio and drew the curtains. Thank God, her heart was all right.

OLD-FASHIONED GENTLEMAN

Once more he picked his brushes from the ginger-jar where in his despair he had thrust them. Nothing in the situation had changed. The fear that Madeleine had lost her love for Phil had never troubled him for an instant. Women's hearts did not beat that way. That Phil's future was assured once he got his feet under him was also a foregone conclusion. What Mr. Eggleston thought about it was another matter, and yet not a serious one. He might be ugly for a time—would be—but that was to be expected in a man who had lost his special capital, a son-in-law and considerable of his reputation at one blow. What had evidently hurt the banker most was the wounding of his pride. He had always stood well with Mr. Stockton—must continue to do so when he realized how many of his other interests depended on his good-will and the trust company's assistance. Phil had not told Adam this when he went over the scene in the office the morning they closed up the accounts, but Gregg had read between the lines. The one bright ray of sunshine was Madeleine's refusal to break her word to her father. That pleased him most of all.

A knock at the door interrupted his revery. It did not sound like Phil's, but Adam had been deceived once before and he hurried to meet him.

This time a messenger stood outside.

"A note for Mr. Adam Gregg," he said. "Are you the man?"

Adam receipted the slip, dismissed the boy and

stepped to the middle of the room under the skylight to see the better. It was from Phil.

"I cannot reach you until late. Have just received a note from the Seaboard Trust Company saying Mr. Stockton wants to see me. More trouble for P. C. & Co., I guess. Hope for good news from Madeleine."

This last note filled his mind with a certain undefined uneasiness. What fresh trouble had arisen? Had some other securities on which money had been loaned—made prior to Phil's awakening—been found wanting in value? He hoped the boy's past wasn't going to hurt him.

With this new anxiety filling his mind he laid down his brushes—he had not yet touched his canvas—put on his hat and strode out into the street. A breath of fresh air would clear his head—it always did.

For two hours he walked the pavements—up through the Park; out along the edge of the river and back again. With every step there came to him the realization of the parallels existing between his own life's romance and that of Philip's. Some of these were mere creations of his brain; others—especially those which ended in the sacrifice of a man's career for what he considered to be right—had a certain basis of fact. Then a shiver crept over him: For honor he had lost the woman he loved: Was Phil to tread the same weary path and for the same cause? And if fate should be thus cruel would he and Madeleine forget in time and lead their lives anew and apart, or would their souls cry out in anguish as his had done all these years, each day bringing a new longing and each day a new pain: he in all the vigor of his manhood and the full flower of his accomplishment and still alone and desolate.

With these reflections, none of them logical—but all showing the perturbed condition of his mind and his anxiety for those he loved, he mounted the stairs of the building and pushed open the door of his studio.

It had grown quite dark and the studio was filled with shadows. As he crossed to the mantel—he rarely entered the room without pausing for a moment in front of the portrait—Olivia's face, with that strange, wan expression which the fading light always brought to view, seemed to stand out from the frame as if in appeal, a discovery that brought a further sinking of the heart to his already overburdened spirit.

With a quick movement, as if dreading the power of prolonged darkness, he struck a match and flashed up the circle of gas jets, flooding the studio with light.

Suddenly he stopped and swept his eyes rapidly around the room. Some one beside himself was present. He had caught the sound of a slight movement and the murmur of whispering voices. Then a low, rippling laugh fell upon his ears—the notes of a bird singing in the dark, and the next instant Madeleine sprang from behind a screen where she had been hiding and threw her arms around his neck.

"Guess!" she cried, pressing his ruddy cheeks, fresh from his walk, between her tiny palms. "Guess what's happened! Quick!"

The revulsion was so great that for the moment he lost his breath.

"No! you couldn't guess! Nobody could. Oh, I'm so happy! *Father's—made—it—up—with—Phil!*"

"Made it up! How do you know?" he stammered.

"Phil's just left him. Come out, Phil!"

Phil's head now peered from behind the screen.

"What do you think of that, Old Gentleman?" he cried, clasping Adam's outstretched hand.

"And there isn't any trouble, Phil, over Mr. Stockton's note?" exclaimed Gregg in a joyous but baffled tone of voice: he was still completely at sea over the situation.

"Trouble over what?" asked Phil, equally mystified.

"That's what I want to know. You wrote me that it meant more trouble for your firm."

"Yes, but that was before I had seen Mr. Stockton. Then I ran across Mr. Eggleston just as he was coming out of the trust company, and he sent me to Madeleine—and we couldn't get here quick enough. She beat me running up your stairs. Hasn't she told you? And you don't know about Stockton's letter? No! Why, he has offered me the position of head of the bond department of the trust company at a salary of ten thousand a year, and I go to work to-morrow! Here's his letter. Let me read you the last clause:"

"No, let me," cried Madeleine, reaching for the envelope.

"It is all her doing, Phil."

OLD-FASHIONED GENTLEMAN

"No—I'll read it," begged Phil.

"No, you won't! I'll read it myself!" burst out Madeleine, catching the letter from Phil's hand and whirling around the room in her glee. "Listen: 'The Trust Company needs men like you, Mr. Colton, and so does the Street!' Isn't that lovely?"

"And that's not all, Old Gentleman!" shouted Phil. "We are going to be married in a month. What do you think of that!"

"And Mr. Eggleston is willing!"

"*Willing!* Why, you don't think he would offend Mr. Stockton, do you?"

Gregg had them in his arms now—Madeleine a bundle of joyous laughter; Phil radiant, self-contained, determined.

For a brief moment the three stood silent. A hush came over them. Adam's head was bent, his forehead almost touching Phil's shoulder, a prayer trembling on his lips. Then with a sudden movement he led them to the portrait, and in an exultant tone, through which an unbidden sob fought its way, he cried:

"Look up, my children—up into your mother's face. See the joy in her eyes! It is all her doing, Phil."

"Oh! my beloved, now you know."

. . . .

The picture has never been taken from Gregg's studio. It still keeps its place over the mantel. There is rarely a day that one of the three does not place flowers beneath it; sometimes Madeleine and Phil ar-

AN OLD-FASHIONED GENTLEMAN

range them; sometimes Adam; and sometimes little blue-eyed, golden-haired Olivia is lifted up in Gregg's strong arms so that she may fill the jar with her own wee hands.

THE END